101
More Training
Games

101
More Training
Games

Gary Kroehnert

The McGraw-Hill Companies, Inc.

Sydney New York San Francisco Auckland
Bangkok Bogotá Caracas Hong Kong
Kuala Lumpur Lisbon London Madrid
Mexico City Milan New Delhi San Juan
Seoul Singapore Taipei Toronto

McGraw·Hill Australia

A Division of The McGraw·Hill Companies

National Library of Australia Cataloguing-in-Publication data:

Kroehnert, Gary.
101 more training games.

ISBN 0 074 70749 3.

1. Management games – Study and teaching. 2. Management games – Study and teaching – Australia. 3. Employees – Training of. 4. Active learning. I. Title. II. Title: One hundred and one more training games.

658.312404

Published in Australia by
McGraw-Hill Book Company Australia Pty Limited
4 Barcoo Street, Roseville NSW 2069, Australia
Acquisitions Editor: Kristen Baragwanath
Production Editor: Sybil Kesteven
Editor: Martin Heng
Designer: R.T.J. Klinkhamer
Illustrator: Diane Booth, Di-Art Design
Cartoonist: Loui Silvestro
Typeset in 10/14 Bell Gothic by R.T.J. Klinkhamer
Printed on 80 gsm woodfree by Best Tri Colour Printing & Packaging Co. Ltd, Hong Kong.

Contents

THE GAMES

CONTENTS

CONTENTS

Introduction

Welcome to my second book of training games. Many readers of the first book, **100 Training Games**, contacted me asking when other books would be coming out. So for them, here is **101 More Training Games**. **102 Extra Training Games** is well under way!

As the Introduction to **100 Training Games** is still current and relevant, I am using it again here with slight modifications. So if you've already read that, skip this and go straight to the games section. The only point to be made before you skip ahead is to let you know that a new category of problem solving has been added. This has been added following readers' requests and now takes the total number of categories to ten. These are now: Icebreaker, Team building, Communication, Facilitator/presentation skills, Mid-course energiser, Problem solving, Learning, Perception, Evaluation and Self-management.

We have all seen and probably participated in various forms of training games, simulations, role-plays, brain teasers, case studies and other related activities. Just because we are aware of them doesn't mean that we can use them any time we wish to.

The use of these activities should allow the participant to discover outcomes, rather than be told everything without trying it. Most of the world's airlines, manufacturing plants, human resource companies, military establishments, small and large companies, private and public organisations now use these forms of structured exercises. The ultimate goal of using these structured exercises should always be improved learning.

Trainers and participants are changing. People attending training courses generally don't want to get involved with exercises that are too 'touchy feely'. Most of the trainers that I know personally don't like using exercises where participants have to stare each other in the eye or start hugging each other. For that reason all of the exercises included in this book are 'hands on' and 'down to earth'.

What these trainers and participants are generally interested in, on top of the information sessions, are structured experiences that they can apply, where no one feels terribly threatened or where they don't have to touch strangers. The other very important criterion that almost everyone agrees to is that the experience should be relevant to the training matter or relevant to the group's requirements.

All facilitators using structured exercises need to be aware that other things may come out in the use of games that normally wouldn't come out using other methods of instruction.

Games, simulations, role-plays, brain teasers, case studies and other related activities have been used successfully in innumerable training situations by a countless number of trainers. We can actually trace the use of games and simulations back thousands of years. Chess is an excellent example of this. Chess was developed in India around the sixth century by the military and was based on solving military problems.

Games, simulations, role-plays, brain teasers, case studies and other related activities have also been used unsuccessfully in countless training situations for many centuries by an untold number of trainers.

For most of us, games, simulations and role-plays were part of the growing-up process. From our earliest school days, we remember playing games such as marbles or hide-and-go-seek. It is now recognised that these games are not only for fun, but also prepare a child for entry into the social system. If any of you took Home Economics, Woodwork or Metalwork at school you would probably call them a simulation of the real workplace. Some of us may also remember when we acted out roles in games such as 'Mothers and Fathers'—another form of role-play.

In a training situation we must be very selective in the use and timing of these methods of instruction. People become bored doing the same thing all the time, even if it is a 'mind-blowing experience' the first few times. If you intend using these methods effectively, plan them into your session notes or your outline.

This book and my previous book, **100 Training Games**, are each aimed at giving both the new and the experienced trainer enough information, samples and sources to carry out competently their function as an adult trainer using these related training activities. They each focus primarily on games and brain teasers, as role plays and case studies have to be designed by the individual trainer for each separate application. I would strongly suggest that new trainers also spend some time looking at my training handbook titled **Basic Training for Trainers** (McGraw-Hill Book Company Australia, 1994).

Today's trainer can simply walk down to the local shopping centre and purchase any number of games over the counter. It's worth mentioning now that even the simplest child's game can have a place in adult education if applied correctly.

Training games are now found in all areas of all kinds of education. It's important that the trainer realises, however, that a game should not be played simply because someone else has said, 'There should be a game played here.'

101 More Training Games will look firstly at the academic differences among games, simulations, brain teasers, role-plays and case studies. It will also address the problem of when to use training games. The largest (and most important) section of the book is a selection of favourite Australian training games and brain teasers. Lastly an updated bibliography is included for new trainers to use as a resource and for further reference.

It's worthwhile noting that trainers and facilitators these days tend to use the terms 'structured experiences' or 'structured exercises' for all of these activities. So when you hear these terms being used you will know that they refer to the same things. For the most part in this book I refer to games, simulations, brain teasers and role-plays as exercises or activities. As far as I am concerned the term used is not that important as long as the trainer knows what the desired outcome is.

Most of the exercises are written as directions, rather than in the third person; however, where necessary I refer to the leader as the facilitator rather than as the trainer. In most structured exercises it's important for the leader not to be a dominant figure. Generally if you use the term 'facilitator' that lets the group know that they aren't going to be taught by a trainer but will rather find out for themselves through experience.

With the exercises contained in this handbook, I would suggest that the reader/user apply commonsense in using the enlarging facilities on their photocopier to make appropriately sized overhead transparencies. This will save presentation time by reducing the writing required on a whiteboard etc.

My policy for reproducing any material from this handbook is based on encouraging interprofessional networking. Therefore the material contained in this book may be freely reproduced for educational purpose or training activities. You are not required to obtain special permission for such uses. It is requested, however, that the following statement appear on all copies made:

Reproduced from:
101 More Training Games, Gary Kroehnert,
McGraw-Hill Book Company Australia, Sydney
Copyright 1999

Finally I would like to thank all of the authors, game designers and publishers who have allowed me to use their material for the benefit of new trainers.

I have attempted to acknowledge sources wherever possible. Where a source hasn't been acknowledged, either the source is unknown to me or my colleagues, or it's an original game design. As it's next to impossible to find the source of a story or game on most occasions, I will now apologise if I have not acknowledged a source or if there are any incorrectly acknowledged.

If you have any games or exercises that you would like to share with other trainers, please send them to me for possible inclusion in future publications (**102 Extra Training Games** is currently under production). Your name will be immortalised forever, as I **will** acknowledge the source. If possible please try to use the same format as shown here. My contact details are shown below.

Before we start looking at the games, just remember what Confucius said around 500 BC.

'I hear and I forget,
I see and I remember,
I do and I understand.'

Have fun!

Dr Gary Kroehnert 1999

PO Box 169
Grose Vale
New South Wales 2753
Australia

Phone: (02) 4572 2000
Fax: (02) 4572 2200
Email: doctorgary@hotmail.com

The Activities

THE DIFFERENCES AMONG THEM ALL

Very few trainers agree on definitions for games, simulations and role-plays, case studies and so on. The following definitions are very broad and are intended for new trainers to use. The more experience a trainer gains, the more they can apply their own definitions.

Even by looking at some of the examples given here, you will see that it's difficult even to categorise some exercises into one grouping. Chess, for example, isn't strictly a game or a simulation; it's a combination of both. For those who are interested chess was developed in sixth-century India and was designed to simulate a contemporary battle.

Games

A game is an exercise where participants are involved in a contest with someone else (or a group of people) with a set of rules imposed. Games normally include some type of pay-off. Most training games are now aimed at having the individual trainee compete with themselves, rather than another trainee. This avoids the situation of having winners and losers.

The term 'games' includes psychomotor skills games, intellectual skills games and most games of chance. Some common types of games include darts, snakes and ladders, football, Scrabble®, charades and most card games. Games in which individuals compete with themselves include solitaire, patience, crossword puzzles and even poker machines.

Simulations

A simulation is a mock-up of an actual or imaginary situation. Simulations are generally used to train future operators where it's impractical or too dangerous for these trainees to use real-life equipment or locations. Simulations are normally designed to be as realistic as possible so that trainees can learn from their actions without the financial worries of repairing or replacing damaged equipment.

Examples of simulations would include flight simulators, driving simulators and war games.

Brain teasers

Brain teasers are in a class of their own. They are neither pure games nor simulations but puzzles that either keep participants' minds busy or highlight key points. Brain teasers generally don't have any rules, but they do allow the trainer to design their own rules to suit the individual training session.

Typical brain teasers include exercises such as joining the dots and most perception exercises.

Role-plays

Role-plays are used in training to see how participants react in certain situations before and after training sessions. Role-plays are very useful in getting participants used to dealing with other people in any given scenario. Even when a participant does it wrong, they still learn.

Case studies

Case studies are exactly what the name implies. A case (normally from the participants' workplace) is studied either by the group or by the individual. An in-depth study of a real-life or simulated scenario is undertaken to illustrate certain outcomes. When the group or the individual comes up with an answer to the problem or situation it can be compared to what really happened and what the outcomes were.

WHEN SHOULD THEY BE USED?

Training exercises may be used at any time during the training session as long as they are relevant to the point or have been designed with a specific purpose.

The 'specific purpose' might be to keep the group occupied while waiting for stragglers or to wake participants up after a lunch break. These purposes are fine as long as they are stated. It's not okay when they are simply used to fill in time or to make the facilitator look like a magician.

You can also use structured exercises as a means of channelling excess energy or to liven up the class. The activity can be a means of improving the learning atmosphere.

So these types of structured exercises should be selected and used on the basis of their usefulness, for reinforcing the instruction, or improving the learning environment.

A FACILITATOR'S RESPONSIBILITIES

Gone are the days when games and the like were not considered suitable as training tools. Training is a serious business, but we can and should use games, simulations, role-plays, brain teasers, case studies and other related activities in training situations.

War games (simulations) have been used by military personnel for many, many centuries and have proved to be very effective. Structured exercises are relatively new to training and they are also proving to be very effective—if used properly.

Regardless of how good we are as presenters or lecturers, we can't fool ourselves into thinking that our presentation alone is going to keep everyone's interest for the entire period. The use of games, simulations, role-plays, brain teasers, case studies and other related activities are all applications of the principles of adult learning. You, the facilitator, must ensure that participants do not become so involved in the activity that they actually miss the learning point. Additionally the facilitator must also realise that if participants have too high a level of enthusiasm for the exercise they may become bored with 'normal' training. This isn't to say that we don't want high levels of enthusiasm, but we need to ensure we keep participants interested with other methods of instruction as well.

The learning process can be sped up by the use of games, simulations, role-plays, brain teasers, case studies and other related activities. People learn better when they are enjoying themselves, so we need to think seriously about creating or supplying the appropriate learning atmosphere.

You should always select the training method after you have set the learning objectives. The method should respond to the participants' needs, not the facilitator's.

When you decide to use a structured exercise it is important to practise the exercise at least once with a group of people not involved with the immediate presentation. This will help you see if the design is going to work—in the expected way with the expected results. Like all types of training, these structured exercises must be evaluated for their worth and effectiveness. If they don't produce what is needed, scrap them or modify them.

Do you have a responsibility for entertaining the group during any presentation? You have the responsibility for ensuring the clarity and precision of information. You are also responsible for aligning the group and keeping it moving. Another responsibility is to keep yourself animated. (That could be considered the main entertainment value.) This is also what the participants may talk about later to their friends and colleagues. If the facilitator is in a situation where this type of feedback is required (as is the case with an external trainer or consultant), then an assortment of training methods is needed. Games, simulations, role plays and structured exercises will be of assistance.

It is your responsibility to pilot or test all new exercises or exercises that you haven't used in the past. Facilitators must realise that what works for some people doesn't always work for others. A lot of training exercises may have different outcomes every time you use them. So be prepared.

Trainers and facilitators must debrief all exercises carried out during any type of training session. The purpose of debriefing is quite complicated. Without going into too much detail there are two main reasons for conducting the debriefing session.

You have an obligation to put the players or participants back together when the exercise has finished. This means that if participants have bad feelings about the exercise they should be allowed to get things off their chest while still in the training room and also while things are still fresh in their minds. You must also put the participants back together if you shatter them or scrape them off the floor.

Debriefing also allows the trainer and the participants to talk about the outcomes of the exercise. Was it what everyone expected? Would you do that in the real situation? What would you have done if this had happened? It also allows the trainer a time where mistakes can be corrected.

Probably your most important responsibility as facilitator is to be completely honest and open with your participants. This includes giving out hidden agendas, not misleading participants, not setting anyone up, not deceiving anyone and not using the participants' efforts for your own gain.

WHERE CAN THEY BE USED?

Rather than fully catalogue these exercises and possibly limit their application, I have decided to use a coding system. Beside the name of the exercises on the following pages you will see one or more of the following letters and symbols. These have been placed there to give you suggested applications. **These applications are only guides and can be modified to suit by the individual trainer.**

Coding:

I   Icebreaker
T   Team building
C   Communication
F   Facilitator/presentation skills
M   Mid-course energiser
X   Problem solving
L   Learning
P   Perception
E   Evaluation
S   Self-management

A full breakdown of the exercises has been included on the next few pages of this handbook. Firstly, each of the ten different categories has been given a detailed overview. The second list is an index of the 101 exercises included in this book, with full cross-referencing for each application for which they can be used.

I Icebreaker

Almost any exercise can be used as an icebreaker. The two main purposes of using icebreakers are, firstly, to allow participants to introduce themselves to each other and, secondly, to lead into the topic matter. Participants often find that the topic matter is made clearer by the use of an appropriate icebreaker.

The exercises in this grouping are non-threatening introductory contacts. They are designed to allow participants to get to know each other a little and to lower any barriers that may exist. Experienced facilitators have found that the success or failure of a program may hinge on these two points.

The more comfortable participants feel with each other, the better the learning environment. If participants feel comfortable with each other, they are more likely to participate and to generate new ideas.

While most facilitators won't see these exercises as too threatening, some participants may. If a participant does see an exercise as threatening, make sure they have a way out of participating. It's a wise move to let people know at the very beginning of a program that they can pass on any exercise or activity they feel uncomfortable with. Obviously there will be exceptions to this. A trainee counsellor, for example, should not be allowed to say that they feel uncomfortable talking with strangers and therefore not have to perform any counselling role-plays. Commonsense rules.

T Team building

Team-building exercises are used to improve the relationship among individuals and subgroups within a group. The term 'group' in team building normally refers to an established work group or a group which will be working together.

When using team-building exercises you, as well as the group, should be aware that the identification of conflict or problems between different parties or individuals may be the only outcome of some team-building exercises. However, a conflict or problem is much easier to solve or deal with after it has been identified. A team-building exercise should allow participants to 'let their hair down' while they get to know each other.

It's very important that you thoroughly debrief team-building exercises to prevent any build-up of hostility, anger or frustration. Don't let the group break until this has been rectified.

C Communication

Exercises used for communication are designed to let participants find out where certain communication skills may be improved. You, as the facilitator, have to be very aware of the exact purpose of some communication exercises as it is sometimes very difficult to sit back and say nothing while things start to go wrong for the participant.

You also need to be aware that you may be looked upon by some participants as a role-model. While conducting a program on communication skills you must ensure that what you give out is correct. As feedback is a very important part of communication skills it must be used in all communication exercises. Feedback should be specific and aimed at observed behaviours that the individual has some control over.

F Facilitator/presentation skills

Facilitation skills are aimed at people who may need to develop or improve their up-front, or presentation, ability. The exercises in this category are designed to get participants thinking about particular aspects of their own presentation and facilitation skills.

While using any exercises to improve presentation skills you should take full advantage of the opportunity by using the individuals in the group wherever possible. This may mean getting some of them to run the exercises. It's important that the facilitator ensures the individuals are observed and debriefed by the rest of the group. By this simple observation group members are able to see things that may or may not work for them. The more styles of presentation they see, the better.

Some of these exercises can be seen as very threatening to a few group members, so make sure you are prepared to offer your support and assistance if necessary.

M Mid-course energiser

Mid-course energisers can be used at any time you observe the group losing interest or falling asleep. Mid-course energisers are very similar in design to icebreakers, but they sometimes make the assumption that group members know each other already. For this reason some of the exercises may appear a little threatening to some members of the group. If someone does not want to participate, let them sit out or act in an observer's role. You will normally find that they join in as soon as they see how much fun the others are having.

These exercise are used to wake participants up, to get the blood moving, to keep participants from falling asleep after a lunch break, to get people back on line or simply to think about a new approach to a problem.

Experienced facilitators can also use these energisers to reduce tensions that may have built up between individuals or within the group.

X Problem solving

Most of the problem-solving exercises have been designed to put participants or small groups in a situation where a solution is expected. These exercises are generally non-threatening.

The solutions that are given may not necessarily be the correct ones, so the facilitator must deal with this. The facilitator must also be aware that the solutions the individuals or groups put forward may actually be better than the one the facilitator had in mind to start with.

Most of the problem-solving exercises also look at the use of synergy within the group. Synergy occurs when the total output of the group is greater than the total combined output of its members.

All problem-solving exercises should be thoroughly debriefed, so that everyone gets to hear other participants' ideas.

L Learning

These exercises are designed to let participants see where their learning styles or attitudes need improvement. They tend to be more experimental in their application. That is, the participants are normally required to do something and come up with some kind of result or answer. After that phase of the exercise the facilitator can normally draw out from the group better ways of doing the same thing with better results.

You must ensure that the whole exercise is totally debriefed and that every participant can see what the final results or methods should be. You should be aware that there are many different learning styles. Don't make the assumption that everyone in the group will learn the same way. Make certain you get plenty of feedback to check participants' understanding.

P Perception

The perception exercises are generally fun for everyone to use. They are designed to see how participants perceive different situations or objects. The end result with most perception exercises is that participants are made aware of their need to use lateral thinking, to look at things in different ways and to try to break down any preconceived stereotypes that they may be using.

As these exercises are fun to use, it is not uncommon to see them being used as icebreakers or mid-course energisers.

Some of the individuals in the group may have difficulty with perception exercises. If so, try to get the rest of the group to explain the different perceptions to them.

E Evaluation

Most of the evaluation exercises are for participants to evaluate either themselves or the program. It is important to point out to participants at the very beginning of the exercise that any evaluation should be constructive, not destructive. Things can be improved or rectified much more easily by using constructive evaluation. Destructive evaluation does nothing but leave ill-feelings with some members.

If any of these exercises are used for the purpose of program evaluation, it's a good idea to make sure participants are told of the results, either verbally or in writing.

S Self-management

Exercises in the category of self-management allow participants to find where they can improve their own self-management techniques. These techniques are the same as time-management techniques, but with a different name. Here we look at improving participants' organisational skills.

Participants get a lot of information and new ideas from other members within the group, so make sure that the whole group finds out what principles each participant used in the exercises.

Games Codes Grid

Game No.	Name	Page	Category	Icebreaker	Team building	Communication	Facilitator/presentation skills	Mid-course energiser	Problem solving	Learning	Perception	Evaluation	Self-management
1	Powers of Concentration	17	ICFMP	●		●	●	●			●		
2	Scrabble®	18	ITMP	●	●			●			●		
3	Roles	20	TCPS		●	●					●		●
4	Letters #1	22	ITMP	●	●			●			●		
5	Stress	24	IMES	●				●				●	●
6	Tell Me About...	26	ICMPLE	●		●		●		●	●	●	
7	Thumbs	27	IMS	●				●					●
8	Egg Ships	28	TCMPLES		●	●		●		●	●	●	●
9	Stress ID	30	IMPES	●				●			●	●	●
10	Q & A	32	ICFMPLE	●		●	●	●		●	●	●	
11	Matches #1	33	IMXLS	●				●	●				●
12	The Moat	34	TCXS		●	●			●				●
13	Expectations	36	ICPES	●		●			●			●	●
14	Objectives	38	IFLE	●			●			●		●	
15	Road Rules	39	ITCFM	●	●	●	●	●					
16	Prepared Sheets	42	IFP	●			●					●	
17	556A	44	ITMP	●	●			●			●		
18	FART	46	FLS				●			●			●
19	The Ping Pong Ball	47	TMXL			●		●	●				
20	Alphabet Soup #1	49	ITM	●	●					●			
21	Population	50	ITCFMXL	●	●	●	●	●	●	●			
22	123 Go	54	ICFMLP	●		●	●	●		●			●
23	More Whispers	55	ITCMLS	●	●	●		●		●			●
24	Uniqueness	56	IT	●	●								
25	Age Split	57	ITM	●	●			●					
26	Break Up	58	ITM	●	●			●					
27	Colour Split	59	ITM	●	●			●					
28	Jigsaw Sort	60	ITM	●	●			●					
29	Morning Tea Cake	61	MX					●	●				
30	Who's With Whom	63	ITCMX	●	●	●		●	●				
31	Finished Early	64	CFMXE			●	●	●	●			●	
32	Impressions	65	ITCMPS	●	●	●		●					●

11

GAME NO. NAME	PAGE	CATEGORY	Icebreaker	Team building	Communication	Facilitator/presentation skills	Mid-course energiser	Problem solving	Learning	Perception	Evaluation	Self-management
33 Rope Circles	67	ITCMXPES	●	●	●		●	●		●	●	●
34 Rope Squares	68	ITCMXPES	●	●	●		●	●		●	●	●
35 Assumptions	69	ICXPS	●		●			●		●		●
36 The Debate	70	ICMLE	●		●		●		●	●	●	
37 Introductions	71	ITL	●	●					●			
38 Taped In	73	TCMX		●	●		●	●				
39 Multiplication	74	XLPE						●	●	●	●	
40 Additions	76	ICFMXLPE	●		●	●	●	●	●	●	●	
41 Notepads	77	TCMXLES		●	●		●	●	●	●	●	●
42 Mix Up	80	ITM	●	●			●					
43 What Is It?	81	ICMXP	●		●		●	●		●		
44 The Circle and the Dot	83	ITMXP	●	●			●	●		●		
45 Magazine Mix Up	85	ITCMXLP	●	●	●		●	●	●	●		
46 Magazine Messages	86	TCMXL		●	●		●	●	●			
47 What Am I?	87	ICMX	●		●		●	●				
48 Top Gun	89	ITCMXLPES	●	●	●		●	●	●	●	●	●
49 Last Will and Testament	90	TLPS		●					●	●		●
50 Winning Points	92	ICMXPES	●		●		●	●		●	●	●
51 How Much Do You Know? #1	93	ITCMXL	●	●	●		●	●	●			
52 Mixed Bits	96	ITCMXLP	●	●	●		●	●	●	●		
53 Missing Numbers #1	98	ITCMXL	●	●	●		●	●	●			
54 Balancing Balls	100	ITCMXL	●	●	●		●	●	●			
55 Mind Reader	102	ICFMP	●		●	●	●			●		
56 My Fantasy	103	ITCMP	●	●	●		●			●		
57 The Orange	105	ICMXPES	●		●		●	●		●	●	●
58 Delegation	106	ICXLPES	●		●			●	●	●	●	●
59 Paperclips	108	ITCMXLPE	●	●	●		●	●	●	●	●	
60 Spot the Flaws	109	ITMXPE	●	●			●	●		●	●	
61 How Much Do You Know? #2	111	ITCMXL	●	●	●		●	●	●			
62 Matches #2	114	IMXLS	●				●	●	●			●
63 Bus Stops	116	ICFMXPS	●		●	●	●	●		●		●
64 What Do We Have Here?	118	IMP	●				●			●		
65 Hidden Phrases	120	ICMX	●		●		●	●				
66 The Interview	122	CMPS			●		●			●		●
67 Team Names	123	ITF	●	●		●						

GAME NO.	NAME	PAGE	CATEGORY	Icebreaker	Team building	Communication	Facilitator/presentation skills	Mid-course energiser	Problem solving	Learning	Perception	Evaluation	Self-management
68	Preconceived	124	CFLP			•	•			•	•		
69	Airport	126	LES							•		•	•
70	Balancing Glasses	127	TMXP		•			•	•		•		
71	How Much Do You Know? #3	129	ITCMXL	•	•	•		•	•	•			
72	Missing Numbers #2	132	ITCMXL	•	•	•		•	•	•			
73	Alphabet Soup #2	134	ITCMX	•	•	•		•	•				
74	PART Game	136	TCFMLPES		•	•	•	•		•	•	•	•
75	Six	142	ICMXLPS	•		•		•	•	•	•		•
76	16 Squares	144	IMP	•				•	•				
77	25 Squares	146	IMP	•				•	•				
78	Triangles	148	IMP	•				•	•				
79	Scavenger Hunt	150	IT	•	•								
80	Likes and Gripes	154	TCXPS		•	•			•		•		•
81	How Much Do You Know? #4	156	ITCMXL	•	•	•		•	•	•			
82	Trodswow	159	IMXPS	•				•	•		•		•
83	Team Effectiveness	161	TXLPES		•				•	•	•	•	•
84	Birthday Card	164	P								•		
85	Card Count	165	TCMXPS		•	•		•	•		•		•
86	Egg Yolks	166	IFMPS	•			•	•			•		•
87	Roving Reporters	168	ITM	•	•			•					
88	Late Starter	169	ITLPE	•	•					•	•	•	
89	Underwater Monument	170	TCXS		•	•			•				•
90	Nines	176	TCXLPS		•	•			•	•	•		•
91	Salt and Pepper	177	ITM	•	•			•					
92	Letters #2	179	IMXP	•				•	•		•		
93	Apples and Oranges	181	MX					•	•				
94	Codewords	183	TX		•				•				
95	Create a Game	186	TFML		•		•	•		•			
96	Chips	189	ITS	•	•								•
97	99.9%	190	IMXPES	•				•	•		•	•	•
98	Missing Numbers #3	192	ITMXLPS	•	•			•	•	•	•		•
99	Errors	194	ICMXS	•		•		•	•				•
100	Trivia of Trivia	196	ITCMXL	•	•	•		•	•	•			
101	Recycled	199	ITCMXLPE	•	•	•		•	•	•	•	•	

The Games

1

Powers of Concentration

ICFMP

TIME REQUIRED	SIZE OF GROUP	MATERIAL REQUIRED
5–10 minutes.	Unlimited.	One sheet of paper for each participant.

Overview

This exercise will show the majority of your participants how individuals perceive information or instructions differently.

Goals

1. To allow participants the experience of receiving instructions that they will have to follow.
2. To allow the group to see how instructions may be interpreted in different ways by different people.

Procedure

1. Give one sheet of paper to each participant.
2. Tell participants that they will be given a set of instructions that they will have to follow. Then tell them that they will have their eyes closed while they are listening to the instructions.
3. After the participants have closed their eyes, give a series of verbal instructions to them. First say, 'I would like you to fold your sheet of paper in half.' When everyone has folded their sheet in half the next instruction is, 'Now tear off the right-hand corner,' followed immediately by, 'Now fold your paper in half again.' When that has been done by all participants again ask them to tear off the right-hand corner and so on. The

facilitator should also be following the instructions being given. (After all, they should know what they mean, shouldn't they?)

4. After all of the instructions have been given to the group ask them to open their eyes and unfold their sheets of paper.
5. Once the group sees the number of different shapes and patterns that have resulted, the facilitator may lead a discussion into the ways of giving and receiving clearer instructions.

Discussion points

1. Why did most people finish up with a different shape to the facilitator?
2. Why did we perform differently to each other?
3. How could we ensure that these instructions could be followed better next time?

Variations

1. Different instructions can be given or the sequencing altered.
2. Jargon could be used (e.g. fold it across the grain).
3. Get the group to perform the exercise a second time after the debriefing has been completed.

TRAINER'S NOTES

2

Scrabble®

ITMP

TIME REQUIRED	SIZE OF GROUP	MATERIAL REQUIRED
30–40 minutes.	Unlimited, but will need to be broken into subgroups of 5–7 people.	None.

Overview

The Scrabble® exercise allows participants to appreciate the value of teamwork and synergy.

Goals

1. To allow participants to discover the value of synergy in problem-solving activities.
2. To allow participants to see how a team will generally come up with a better result than a series of individuals.

Procedure

1. Inform the group that they will be going through a problem-solving activity. They will be required to come up with one answer individually, then form groups to come up with a group solution.
2. Ask the participants to write the letters of the alphabet (A to Z) down the left-hand side of a sheet of paper. Then ask them individually to write the designated value of each letter in the game called Scrabble®. Allow 3–4 minutes for this.
3. When all participants have completed this phase, ask them to form groups of 5–7 people. These groups should now discuss the individual results and come up with a group answer. Allow 10–15 minutes for this phase.
4. After all groups have completed their discussions, the facilitator should get them to post their suggested values on the whiteboard. This should be broken into two columns, one for individual values and one for group values.
5. The facilitator can now lead a discussion into the value of teamwork and synergy for problem-solving activities.

Discussion points

1. Why were the majority of the group values significantly closer to being correct?
2. How many sets of individual values were closer than the group values?
3. How can we apply these findings in the workplace?

Variations

1. Use one larger group instead of smaller groups.
2. Impose a tighter time frame.
3. Conduct the exercise non-verbally.

TRAINER'S NOTES

Scrabble® values

A—1	B—3	C—3	D—2	E—1	F—4
G—2	H—4	I—1	J—8	K—5	L—1
M—3	N—1	O—1	P—3	Q—10	R—1
S—1	T—1	U—1	V—4	W—4	X—8
Y—4	Z—10				

© 1999 GARY KROEHNERT. 101 MORE TRAINING GAMES.

3

Roles

TIME REQUIRED	SIZE OF GROUP	MATERIAL REQUIRED
30–60 minutes.	Unlimited, but will need to be broken into subgroups of 5–7 people.	A prepared 'Roles' overhead and a sheet of paper and pen for each participant.

Overview

This exercise leads participants to re-examine their job roles and responsibilities. It may also be used to conduct a task breakdown.

Goals

1. To allow participants to see how they fit into their position.
2. To examine participants' responsibilities.
3. To clarify a particular position's responsibilities.
4. To conduct a task breakdown.

Procedure

1. Introduce the idea that all positions within organisations are constantly changing. Also suggest that sometimes the organisational chart or matrix with which we are all familiar may not be the best way to establish a position's roles and responsibilities.
2. Ask the group to consider a new form of matrix with them in the middle, then show them the Roles overhead.
3. Explain to the group that they should place their name in the centre of their sheet of paper and then include all of the people, groups, organisations etc., that they interact with. More circles can be added if required.

4. After the group have listed this information ask them to form groups of 5–7 people and discuss their Roles sheets with the other group members. Suggestions for modifications, additions and deletions should be encouraged.
5. On completion of the discussion ask the participants to rank each entry in order of importance to their position. This will allow participants to set up an action plan to improve relationships in certain areas if needed.
6. It may also be useful to suggest to participants that they talk with their supervisors about these results when they get back to their workplace to clarify any misunderstandings.

Discussion points

1. Did you find your position to be more complex than you imagined?
2. Is it easier to appreciate your role and responsibilities with this type of chart?
3. Do you need to improve relationships in the higher priority areas?

Variations

1. Supervisors may examine positions they are responsible for using this exercise.
2. This exercise can be used to conduct task breakdowns.

TRAINER'S NOTES

Roles

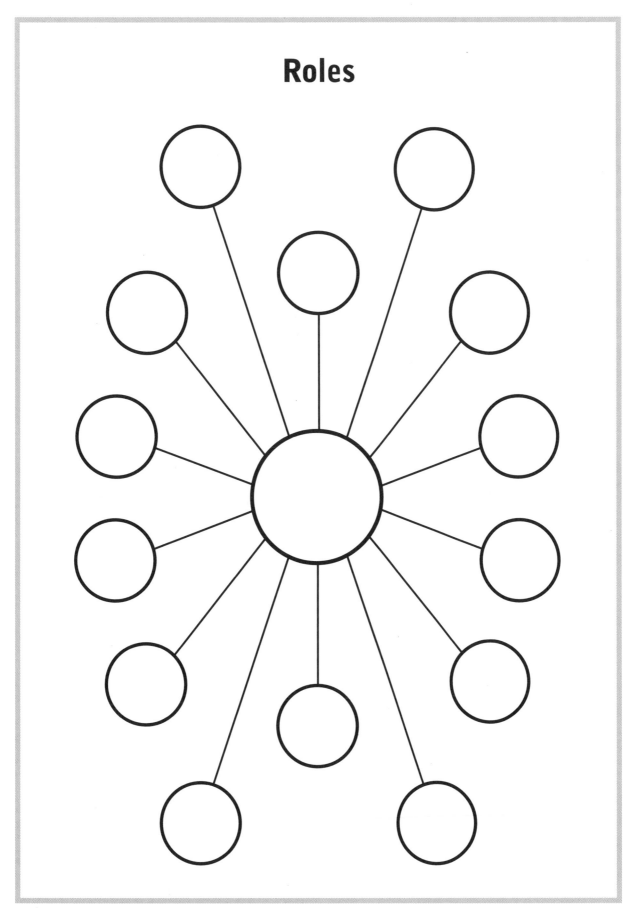

4

Letters #1

ITMP

TIME REQUIRED	SIZE OF GROUP	MATERIAL REQUIRED
30–60 minutes.	Unlimited, but will need to be broken into subgroups of 5–7 people.	A prepared 'Letters' overhead and a pen and paper for each participant.

Overview

This exercise gives participants a chance to work first as individuals, then in small groups. It can be focused on teamwork or synergy.

Goals

1. To allow participants to see the effects of synergy.
2. To develop teamwork.
3. To energise the group.

Procedure

1. Ask participants to write the letters of the alphabet down the left-hand side of a sheet of paper.
2. Now ask them to write the name of the workshop/course beside the letters of the alphabet that they have just written. The facilitator may need to add in extra words to take the title to 26 letters or more in total (part words are okay). An example of this would be 'The XYZ Workshop for Salespers' (26 letters). Each letter of the alphabet should now have another letter beside it. All participants should have the same letters on their sheets.
3. Ask the participants to look at the pairs of letters they now have and think of famous people who have those initials. Their task is to individually list down (on their sheets beside the letters) as many famous people as they can in 5 minutes.
4. After this phase has been completed get the totals from each of the individuals and list them on the board.

5. Now ask the participants to form subgroups of 5–7 and give them another 5 minutes to perform the same task. They should work together within their groups and share ideas.
6. After the groups have finished retrieve the group scores and show them on the board next to the individual scores. Lead into a discussion as to why the group scores are significantly better than the individual scores.

Discussion points

1. Why are the group scores better than the individual scores?
2. Was it easier to find names as a group as opposed to doing it by yourself? Why?
3. How many people limited each pair of initials to one answer (self-imposed rules)? Why?

Variations

1. Company names or product titles may be used in place of the workshop name.
2. After the small groups have given their scores another step could be added to allow the total group 5 more minutes to complete the task again. This will generally give better results again, but will lead into discussions about what size group is most manageable.

Example used

A	T
B	H
C	E
D	X
E	Y
F	Z
.	.
.	.
.	.
U	E
V	S
W	P
X	E
Y	R
Z	S

TRAINER'S NOTES

Letters

```
A   T
B   H
C   E
D   X
E   Y
F   Z
.   .
.   .
.   .
U   E
V   S
W   P
X   E
Y   R
Z   S
```

Stress

IMES

TIME REQUIRED	SIZE OF GROUP	MATERIAL REQUIRED
10–15 minutes.	Unlimited.	A prepared 'Stress' overhead and a pen and paper for each participant.

Overview

This exercise allows participants to identify where they feel stress in their body.

Goal

1. To allow participants to feel where their stress is located.

Procedure

1. Tell the participants that they will have 60 seconds to prepare for a 5-minute presentation about themselves.
2. After the 60 seconds inform the group that they will not have to give this presentation. The purpose of putting them through this scenario was to let them feel some stress.
3. Now ask the group to draw their body on a sheet of paper and to shade in the areas where they felt stress.

4. After everyone has drawn and shaded their bodies ask the group where they all felt it. Note the similarities and the differences.
5. Lead into a discussion on how to deal with stress.

Discussion points

1. Where did everyone feel their stress?
2. How do you currently deal with stress?
3. Is all stress bad for us?

Variations

1. Handouts of prepared drawings can be given out to save time drawing bodies.
2. Small groups can be formed to identify where they all felt stress.
3. Coloured pencils could be used to identify common areas of stress and areas of high stress.

TRAINER'S NOTES

Stress

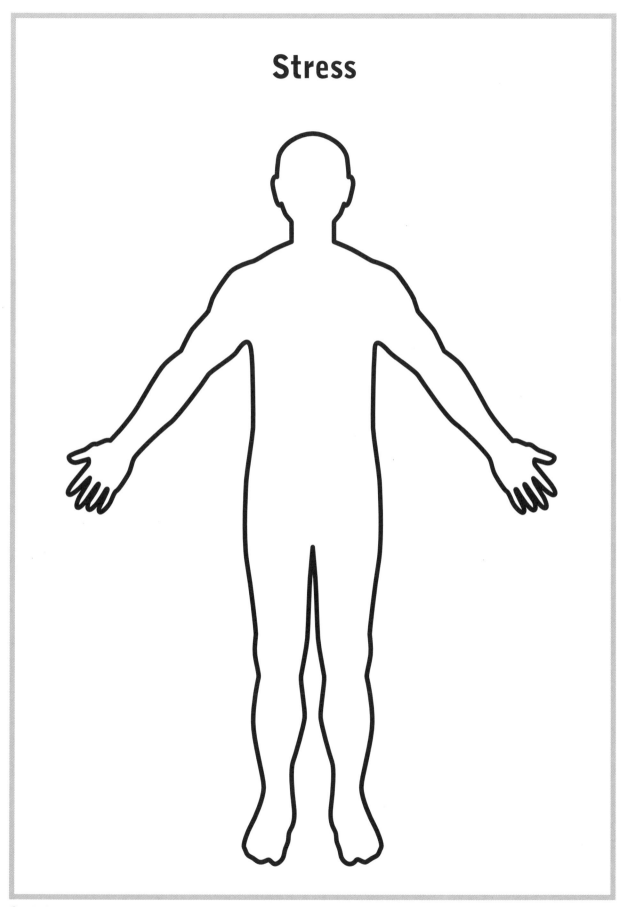

Tell Me About ...

ICMPLE

TIME REQUIRED	SIZE OF GROUP	MATERIAL REQUIRED
10 minutes plus discussion time.	Unlimited.	Sufficient sheets of flip-chart paper and markers.

Overview

An exercise to get participants to identify which topics/subjects they need more information on.

Goals

1. To allow participants to identify what information they lack.
2. To get the participants moving around.

Procedure

1. Tell the group that they are going to have 10 minutes to identify other topics, subjects, questions or concerns about which they would like to have more information. Once they have identified these things, they are to write them on the flip-chart paper so that the facilitator may give the requested information or make suitable arrangements.

2. After the group have finished writing the facilitator then takes each point listed in turn and gives the information, answers the question or deals with the comment in some other way.

Discussion point

1. At the conclusion the facilitator should ask if any further concerns have been raised by the discussion.

Variation

1. A number of sheets may be used with different headings on each. For example:
   'What questions would I like to ask?'
   'What concerns do I have now?'
   'What else do I need to know about?'
   'Please tell me more about ...'

TRAINER'S NOTES

7

Thumbs

IMS

TIME REQUIRED	SIZE OF GROUP	MATERIAL REQUIRED
5 minutes.	Unlimited.	None.

Overview

This quick exercise shows participants how a new way of doing something may feel uncomfortable.

Goals

1. To allow participants to see that old ways are generally more comfortable.
2. To discuss how a new way may become a habit.

Procedure

1. Ask the individuals in the group to clasp their hands together.
2. Now ask them to look at **how** they have clasped their hands together. If they have their left thumb on top of the right, they are to unclasp their thumbs and fingers and interlace them the opposite way. This would mean that their right thumb is now on top and all of the fingers have changed as well.
3. Ask the group if that feels as comfortable as the other way around. Most people will say that it feels uncomfortable.
4. Ask the group if they think it will start to feel more comfortable if they keep doing it this new way all the time. Will the old way start to feel uncomfortable?
5. Now ask the group to unclasp their hands. You can now state that some of the things to be dealt with during this program may feel a little uncomfortable. However, if they persevere with the new way, it will become the normal, comfortable way of doing things.
6. The last point to be made is that when we are placed under pressure we often revert to the old ways because they tend to be quicker. We must avoid this as the old habits will never die if we keep using them.

Discussion points

1. Why do we revert to old habits?
2. How can we develop new habits?

Variations

1. Folding arms can be used instead of clasping hands.
2. Writing a word with the non-preferred hand can also be used as an alternative.

TRAINER'S NOTES

8

Egg Ships

TCMPLES

TIME REQUIRED	SIZE OF GROUP	MATERIAL REQUIRED
75–90 minutes.	Unlimited, but needs to be broken into subgroups of 5–7 people.	One raw egg, one roll of sticky tape, sufficient drinking straws and marking pens for each subgroup. Spare eggs are advisable. A briefing sheet is included should you wish to distribute a copy to each group.

Overview

This exercise is designed to involve participants in a number of issues such as problem solving, team building, teamwork, customer service skills etc.

Goals

1. To allow participants to identify some strategies in customer service.
2. To allow participants to practise some problem-solving techniques.

Procedure

1. Participants form subgroups of 5–7 people. Tell the groups that they represent companies that produce spacecraft. These companies will be competing for a lucrative contract to construct a particular type of craft for the next decade.
2. Each group has the task of designing, constructing and evaluating a spacecraft suitable for the transportation of raw eggs. Give them 45 minutes to design and construct their Egg Ships using the materials supplied.
3. At the end of the construction phase, tell the groups that there will be a two-part evaluation, each consisting of a test flight. Should the eggs break during either test flight the company will be sued for damages.
4. The first part of the evaluation will consist of a 1-metre test flight. The Egg Ships will be held 1 metre above ground level and dropped to the

floor. The egg must not break during this test flight.
5. The second part of the evaluation will be a 5-metre test flight. The Egg Ships will be located 5 metres above ground level and dropped to the floor. Again the eggs must not break.
6. When the evaluation phase is completed a discussion may be led into problem-solving strategies, teamwork, customer service skills etc.

Discussion points

1. Which teams passed both of the evaluation criteria?
2. What was the problem? How was it broken down? Who did what?
3. Did any group ask the customer for more specific details such as the required colour, company logos etc? Why? Why not?
4. Did any group get the customer involved in the process? Why? Why not?

Variations

1. Sticks may be used instead of straws.
2. Boiled eggs may be used to save cleaning up if any happen to break.
3. Different coloured straws and pens can be given to each group.
4. Materials may be unevenly distributed among the groups.

TRAINER'S NOTES

Egg Ships

Your team represents a company that designs, builds and flies custom-built spacecraft. You will be competing for a lucrative contract to design and construct Egg Ships for the next decade.

For this exercise you will have 45 minutes to design your Egg Ship. On completion of the design and construction your Egg Ship will be evaluated and put through two separate test flights. Should the egg break during either test flight the company will be sued for damages.

The first test flight will be a 1-metre flight. The Egg Ship must be held 1 metre above ground level and dropped to the floor. The egg must not break during this flight.

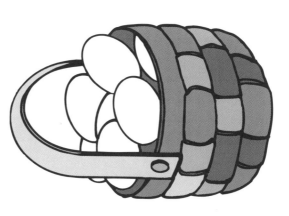

The second test flight will be a 5-metre flight. The Egg Ship will be located 5 metres above ground level and dropped to the floor. Again the egg must not break.

All of the raw material (pun definitely intended) will be distributed by your customer.

Good luck!

9

Stress ID

IMPES

TIME REQUIRED	SIZE OF GROUP	MATERIAL REQUIRED
5–10 minutes.	Unlimited.	A prepared 'Stress ID' overhead and a pen and paper for each participant.

Overview

This exercise is similar to 'Stress' (Game 5), but not as threatening. It allows participants to identify where they feel stress in their body.

Goal

1. To allow participants to feel where their stress is located.

Procedure

1. Ask the individuals within the group to draw a body and shade in where they usually feel stress.
2. After everyone has drawn and shaded their bodies ask the group where they all felt it. Note the similarities and the differences.

3. This can now lead into a discussion on how to deal with stress.

Discussion points

1. Where does everyone feel their stress?
2. How do you currently deal with stress?
3. Is all stress bad for us?

Variations

1. Handouts of prepared drawings can be given out to save time drawing bodies.
2. Small groups can be formed to identify where they all feel stress.
3. Coloured pencils could be used to identify common areas of stress and areas of high stress.

TRAINER'S NOTES

Stress ID

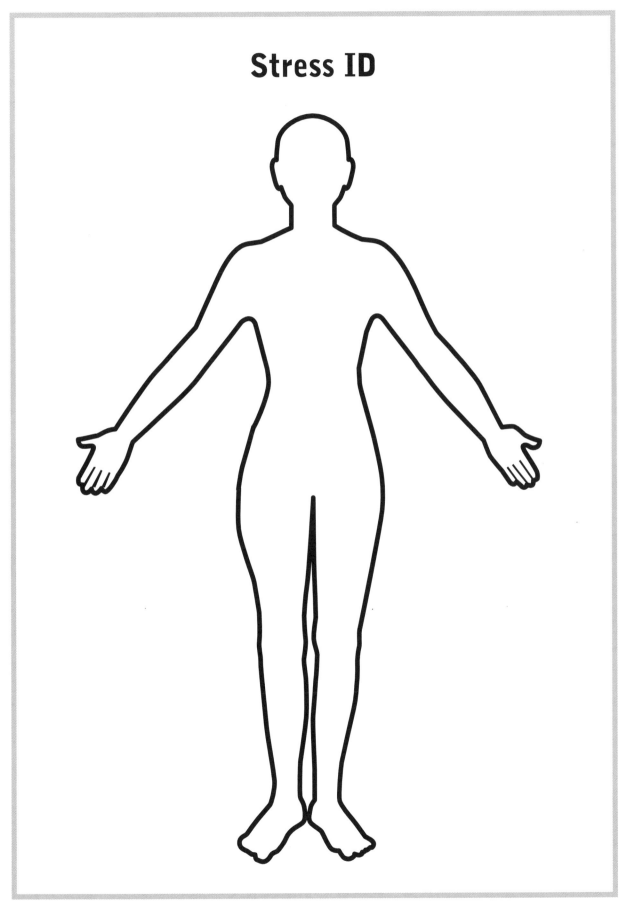

10

Q & A

TIME REQUIRED	**SIZE OF GROUP**	**MATERIAL REQUIRED**
20–30 minutes.	Unlimited, but needs to be broken into subgroups of 5–7 people.	Sufficient flip-chart paper and markers for each group.

Overview

Q & A allows individuals to formulate questions for the facilitator to deal with.

Goals

1. To allow group members an opportunity to ask questions.
2. To get group members working together on problems and perhaps stimulate them to come up with some solutions.

Procedure

1. Participants form groups of 5–7.
2. Tell participants that, within their subgroups, they will be required to formulate questions relating to the course. These questions should be written on the flip-chart paper provided to each group. Approximately 15 minutes should be allowed for this.
3. After all groups have formulated their questions, post them on the wall. Deal with each of the questions in turn.

Discussion points

1. Have all of your questions now been answered?
2. Have any other questions now come to mind?

Variations

1. If a large number of questions is raised and time is limited, they may be prioritised by the group as a whole and only the highest on the list dealt with.
2. The questions may be handed back to the group (or subgroups) for them to find their own answers if time permits.
3. See if the questions from one subgroup can be answered by participants from others.

TRAINER'S NOTES

11
Matches

IMXLS

TIME REQUIRED	SIZE OF GROUP	MATERIAL REQUIRED
10–15 minutes.	Unlimited.	Six matchsticks for each participant.

Overview

An exercise in lateral thinking and problem solving.

Goals

1. To allow participants direct experience of problem solving.
2. To allow participants direct experience of lateral thinking.
3. To highlight the value of working with others in a team situation (synergy).

Procedure

1. Give each participant 6 matches.
2. Ask them to construct 4 triangles with the 6 matches provided without breaking any of them. Give them 2–3 minutes to complete the problem.
3. Allow participants to lead a discussion into the strategies they used to solve this problem. This should lead into a discussion of lateral thinking and the use of other people's ideas (i.e. teamwork).

Discussion points

1. How many people found a solution?
2. How many people found more than one solution?
3. Why do most people place limitations on solutions? (For example, limiting themselves to having all matches flat on the table.)

Variations

1. This exercise may be conducted in small groups.
2. Use other thin, straight items, such as drinking straws, but inform participants that they cannot be bent.

Solution

TRAINER'S NOTES

12

The Moat

TCXS

TIME REQUIRED	SIZE OF GROUP	MATERIAL REQUIRED
Variable.	Unlimited, but needs to be broken into subgroups of 5–7 participants.	Eight stakes for each group. Two pieces of timber for each group (50 mm x 100 mm x 2000 mm). Overhead transparency of The Moat. Two sheets of paper or board and one roll of masking tape or coloured tape.

Overview

An exercise in teamwork and lateral thinking in which participants are given a task to perform. This exercise can be conducted outdoors very effectively.

Goals

1. To allow participants direct experience of teamwork.
2. To introduce lateral thinking.

Procedure

1. Participants form subgroups of 5–7 members.
2. Now give the groups their briefing. Each group has been asked to rescue someone who is being held captive inside a castle. Unfortunately, the castle is sitting on a square island with a 2.1-metre wide, crocodile-infested moat around it. The only way to access the island is with the drawbridge—and it has been raised to stop your rescue operation. You have searched the area and found two planks. These planks are the ONLY items available to you.

3. Your task is to get to the island safely and rescue the person being held captive. The problem is, how are you going to cross the crocodile-infested moat? If you touch the water you can assume you have been eaten and your rescue attempt has failed!

Discussion points

1. How long did it take to come up with a solution?
2. Is this the only solution?
3. What was the process?
4. How may this apply to everyday situations?

Variations

1. This activity may be used either indoors or outdoors. If used outdoors make sure you use your imagination when creating the moat!
2. Other stories may be used, but employ creativity in your choice.

TRAINER'S NOTES

1. Ensure everything is prepared before this activity is introduced, including the tape on the floor.
2. Each group should be far enough apart to ensure ideas aren't copied.

One solution is:

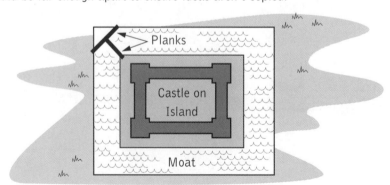

The Moat

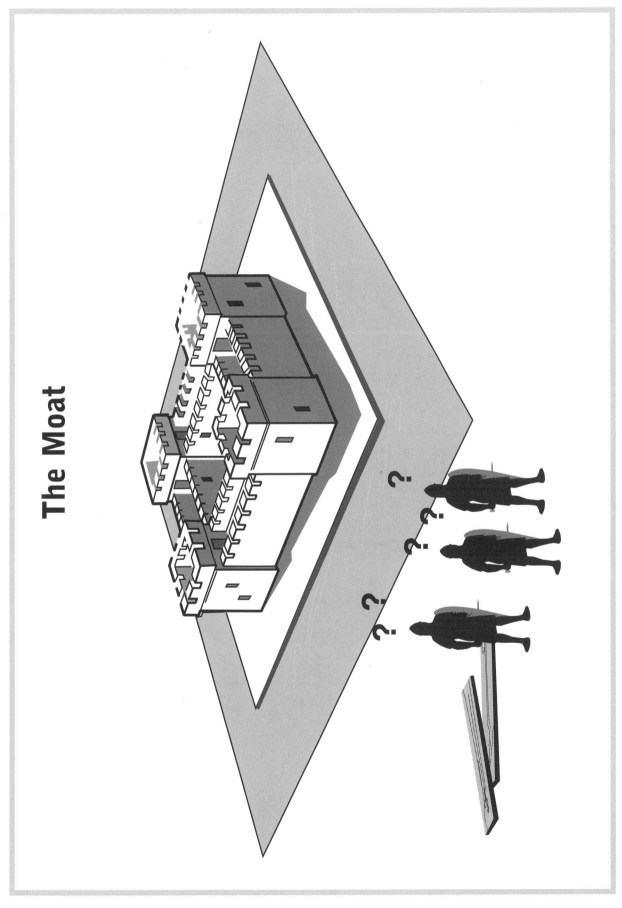

13

Expectations

TIME REQUIRED	SIZE OF GROUP	MATERIAL REQUIRED
20–30 minutes.	Unlimited.	A prepared overhead transparency or flip-chart with questions displayed. Pen and paper for each participant. A sheet of flip-chart paper and marker for each small group.

Overview

This activity has been designed to get participants to focus on their expected outcomes for the session.

Goals

1. To allow participants to identify their requirements from the session.
2. To focus the facilitator on both group and individual needs.

Procedure

1. Begin the session by introducing yourself to the group.
2. Then give the participants a sheet of paper and a pen and ask them to answer the prepared questions. Allow about 5 minutes.
3. After all participants have completed the task individually, ask them to form small groups of 5–7 members. These groups should discuss each of the individual responses and make a combined list on a sheet of flip-chart paper.
4. When completed, all the flip-chart sheets are posted around the room.

5. Advise participants that it is up to them to ensure all of these responses are dealt with during the session. (However, the facilitator should also ensure that all responses are dealt with.)

Discussion points

1. Are all of the points raised relevant?
2. Do we have enough time to cover everything?
3. Should we prioritise the points/issues?

Variations

1. The small group component may be deleted.
2. Questions may be modified to suit group/topic needs.
3. Questions 2, 3 and 4 may be deleted.

Expectations (see also following page)

1. What do I/we want from this course?
2. One thing I hope will happen is ...
3. One thing I hope won't happen is ...
4. I will know the course has been successful if ...

TRAINER'S NOTES

Expectations

1. What do I/we want from this course?

2. One thing I hope will happen is ...

3. One thing I hope won't happen is ...

4. I will know the course has been successful if ...

14

Objectives

IFLE

TIME REQUIRED	SIZE OF GROUP	MATERIAL REQUIRED
10 minutes.	Unlimited.	Paper and pen for each person.

Overview

This activity allows participants to focus on what they would like to get from the program.

Goals

1. To allow participants to set their own learning objectives.
2. To set in place a simple method of evaluation.

Procedure

1. Ask the individuals in the group to take 5 minutes to write down their individual objectives for the program on their sheet of paper. These objectives should relate to issues or topics that they would like to explore during the course.
2. After everyone has completed this part of the activity tell them that it is now their responsibility to ensure that the objectives they identified are met.

3. At the end of the course get everyone to find their written objectives and check to see that they have been met. If not, they may be dealt with at this stage.

Discussion points

1. Did everyone have objectives before they came?
2. Do your objectives realistically link in with the program?

Variations

1. After everyone has written their objectives down, you may wish to collect them to list in a prominent place.
2. The activity can be used as an icebreaker by conducting it in small groups.

TRAINER'S NOTES

15

Road Rules

ITCFM

TIME REQUIRED	SIZE OF GROUP	MATERIAL REQUIRED
30–40 minutes.	Unlimited, but needs to be broken into subgroups of 5–7.	A copy of the 'Road Rules Quiz Sheet'.

Overview

This exercise gives groups the opportunity to find out for themselves some of the values in teamwork.

Goals

1. To get participants involved in a team-building activity.
2. To get participants thinking of ways to improve teamwork and communication in their own areas.

Procedure

1. Give each participant a copy of the 'Road Rules Quiz Sheet'.
2. Ask participants to put their individual answers in the left-hand column on the score sheet. This phase of the exercise is to be done in silence.
3. After everyone has completed their individual answers get the larger group to break into subgroups of 5–7 people. These subgroups are now required to come up with group solutions to the questions. One person from each group should record the group's answers in the right-hand column of the score sheet.
4. When all groups have completed the exercise give out the correct answers along with the number of points awarded for each correct response.

5. Post the final individual scores and the final group scores for comparison (a suggested format is shown).
6. When the group has had a chance to compare the performances for themselves lead the discussion into why the team scores were generally better than most individual scores.

Discussion points

1. Did the teams perform better than the individuals?
2. Did anyone **not** learn anything regarding the rules of the road from this exercise?
3. Were the team scores significantly better than the individual scores?
4. Why were the team scores better?

Variations

1. Set a time limit.
2. Use one very large group.
3. Use any set of rules that the whole group can be expected to know.

TRAINER'S NOTES

This exercise will have to be rewritten for different states and countries.

Road Rules Quiz Sheet

	Individual answers	Score	Group answers	Score	
1. What is the maximum speed for the holder of:					
(a) a learner's permit?	(a)		(a)		
(b) a provisional licence?	(b)		(b)		
2. How many points can be lost for:					
(a) exceeding the speed limit by more than 45 km/h?	(a)		(a)		
(b) not making a U-turn safely?	(b)		(b)		
(c) not wearing a seat belt?	(c)		(c)		
(d) negligent driving?	(d)		(d)		
3. How many glasses of table wine are equivalent to three middies (or 285 ml) of beer?					
4. Draw the sign that indicates there is a roundabout ahead.					
5. What is the meaning of a zig-zag line painted on the road?					
6. What does a flashing yellow light indicate at a pelican crossing?					
7. Draw the sign that indicates a speed zone ceases and that a limit of 100 km/h applies.					
8. How close can you park to another vehicle when parked parallel to the kerb?					
9. How close can you park to:					
(a) a postbox	(a)		(a)		
(b) a railway crossing on the approach side?	(b)		(b)		
(c) a bus stop on the approach side?	(c)		(c)		
(d) any double centre lines marked on the roadway?	(d)		(d)		
10. What does an 'R' endorsement on a driving licence indicate?					
		Total		Total	

Road Rules Quiz—Answers

		Score
1. What is the maximum speed for the holder of: (a) a learner's permit? (b) a provisional licence?	(a) 80 km/h (b) 80 km/h	1 point 1 point
2. How many points can be lost for: (a) exceeding the speed limit by more than 45 km/h? (b) not making a U-turn safely? (c) not wearing a seat belt? (d) negligent driving?	(a) 6 points (b) 2 points (c) 3 points (d) 3 points	1 point 1 point 1 point 1 point
3. How many glasses of table wine are equivalent to three middies (or 285 ml) of beer?	3 glasses	1 point
4. Draw the sign that indicates there is a roundabout ahead.		2 points
5. What is the meaning of a zig-zag line painted on the road?	Pedestrian crossing ahead.	1 point
6. What does a flashing yellow light indicate at a pelican crossing?	You may drive through carefully if there is no risk of colliding with a pedestrian.	1 point
7. Draw the sign that indicates a speed zone ceases and that a limit of 100 km/h applies.		2 points
8. How close can you park to another vehicle when parked parallel to the kerb?	1 metre	1 point
9. How close can you park to: (a) a postbox (b) a railway crossing on the approach side? (c) a bus stop on the approach side? (d) any double centre lines marked on the roadway?	(a) 3 metres (b) 20 metres (c) 20 metres (d) 3 metres	1 point 1 point 1 point 1 point
10. What does an 'R' endorsement on a driving licence indicate?	May also ride any motor cycle.	2 points

Note: Answers based on 1997 edition of the New South Wales Motor Handbook.

	Possible Total	20 points

16

Prepared Sheets

IFP

TIME REQUIRED	SIZE OF GROUP	MATERIAL REQUIRED
No extra time required.	Unlimited.	Prepared flip-chart sheets.

Overview

A way of eliciting more ideas/answers from participants than they would normally have developed.

Goal

1. To encourage participants to come up with a maximum number of ideas/answers.

Procedure

1. Any activity requiring groups to use flip-chart paper may incorporate this format.
2. After a group has been asked to list ideas/items/answers on the flip-chart paper, simply give them one or more of the prepared sheets. No explanation is required. (It should encourage them to put at least one idea in each part.)

Discussion points

1. Did this format limit the number of ideas/answers?
2. Discussion may lead to lateral thinking if required.

Variations

1. Design your own patterns.
2. The 'Prepared Sheets' may be given to individuals rather than small groups. If used this way, prepare handouts for participants beforehand.

TRAINER'S NOTES

Prepared Sheets

17

556A

ITMP

TIME REQUIRED	SIZE OF GROUP	MATERIAL REQUIRED
15–20 minutes.	Unlimited, but needs to be broken into subgroups of 5–7 people.	A copy of the '556A Question Sheet' either as a handout or as an overhead transparency.

Overview

This quick exercise will allow individuals to see the benefit of working together during the program.

Goals

1. To allow participants to see the benefit of working together to achieve better results.
2. To allow participants to see the value of joint problem-solving methods.

Procedure

1. Advise the group that they are going to be given a quick quiz to complete.
2. Give each participant a copy of the '556A Question Sheet' and tell them that they are to answer as many questions as possible by themselves on the sheet in 2 minutes.
3. After the 2 minutes have passed, get the group to form smaller groups of 5–7 people. Give these subgroups 5 minutes to arrive at a set of answers on which everyone agrees.
4. The subgroups now give their answers to all of the questions. Keep the pace up during this phase. Give the answers to any questions that the groups have not been able to answer correctly.
5. You can summarise the activity simply by saying, 'If everyone participates in the upcoming activities and discussions on this program you can see from this exercise that we will achieve far better results.' Alternatively, a discussion may be led into problem-solving strategies or synergy.

Discussion points

1. Why were the group scores higher than the individual scores?
2. Did anyone **not** learn anything new?
3. How can we use joint problem-solving methods on this course or in the workplace?

Variations

1. Questions may be placed on an overhead transparency.
2. Questions may be rewritten using other material. A diverse range of topic areas is important if you make up your own quiz.
3. Teams can compete with a time limit imposed.

Answers

1. Where a person is found guilty of an offence but no criminal record of the conviction is made
2. Yellow
3. Susie Maroney
4. 10 dollars
5. Richard Nixon
6. Colleen McCullough
7. Eleven
8. Socrates
9. A fern
10. Ichi

TRAINER'S NOTES

Some questions may need to be rewritten for different countries.

556A Question Sheet

1. In Australia what is a 'Section 556A' under the **Crimes Act 1900**?

2. Which colour jersey is traditionally worn by the overall leader in a multistage bicycle road-race?

3. Which Australian swimmer made a double crossing of the English Channel in July 1991?

4. Which denomination Australian banknote has a picture of architect Francis Greenway on one side and author/poet Henry Lawson on the other side?

5. Who was U.S. president in 1973?

6. Who was the author of **The Thornbirds**?

7. How many players are there in a soccer team?

8. Which Greek philosopher lived from 470–399 B.C.?

9. What is a **Nephrolepis**?

10. How do you say the number 'one' in Japanese?

18

FART

TIME REQUIRED	SIZE OF GROUP	MATERIAL REQUIRED
5 minutes.	Unlimited.	A whiteboard and marker **or** a flip-chart sheet and marker **or** an overhead transparency.

Overview

An activity that may be included in any time management or supervision course to show participants different options when dealing with paperwork.

Goal

1. To allow participants to remember the options available to them when dealing with paperwork—in a humorous way.

Procedure

1. During any form of time management or supervision course the facilitator may introduce this activity.
2. Inform the group that they have four options available to them after paperwork has been sorted. Ask the group what these options are, one at a time.
3. As the options are given, list them on the whiteboard, flip-chart or overhead transparency and, if necessary, alter the answers given to make them more appropriate (e.g. RAFT).
4. After all four have been given and discussed, inform the group of the easy way to remember them—simply highlight the mnemonic:

F   File it
A   Act on it
R   Refer/delegate it
T   Throw it!

Discussion point

1. All four points are briefly discussed as they are raised.

Variation

1. It may be necessary with some groups to use the mnemonic RAFT—but it won't achieve the same retention!

TRAINER'S NOTES

19

The Ping Pong Ball

TMXL

TIME REQUIRED	SIZE OF GROUP	MATERIAL REQUIRED
Variable.	Unlimited, but best if broken into small groups of 5–7 members.	Each group will require all of the items listed below or, at the very least, a good imagination, perhaps with the use of the overhead transparency supplied.

Overview

An interesting and thought-provoking activity designed to get participants working together.

Goals

1. To get participants to work together.
2. To develop lateral thinking.
3. To look at the benefits of synergy.

Procedure

1. Show the participants a steel pipe which has been embedded in a slab of concrete. The pipe has an internal diameter 3 mm larger than a ping pong ball. The pipe is projecting 300 mm from the ground.
2. Tell them that a ping pong ball has been dropped into the pipe. Their task is to retrieve the ping pong ball without damaging it or the pipe. They have searched the area and found the following items. They may use any or all of these items to assist them with their task.
3. After the activity has been completed a discussion should follow on solutions and strategies used.

Discussion points

1. How many solutions were found? Will they all work?
2. Did the group develop ideas in addition to the individuals' solutions? Why? Why not?
3. How can this activity be related to everyday activities?

Variations

1. Substitute items may be used.

2. This activity may be divided into two parts, having individual participants find their own solution then having them come up with group solutions.

Items found for use

1 large shifter
1 carpenter's saw
1 ball of string
1 small jar of honey
2 sheets of writing paper
2 pens
1 pair of reading glasses
1 unopened can of soft drink
1 plastic shower screen
1 tennis ball
2 rolls of toilet paper
1 unopened bottle of wine
2 ceramic cups
4 unused party balloons
2 raw eggs
1 small chili plant

Possible solutions

1. Pour the soft drink and/or the wine into the pipe to make the ping pong ball float to the top.
2. Put some honey on the end of the string and use that to lift the ping pong ball out of the pipe.
3. Get some chilies off the chili plant, dry out the seeds, put them in the pipe, water them and let them grow. The new plant will lift the ping pong ball out of the pipe.
4. Everyone can pee in the pipe.
5. And many many other solutions.

TRAINER'S NOTES

Items Found

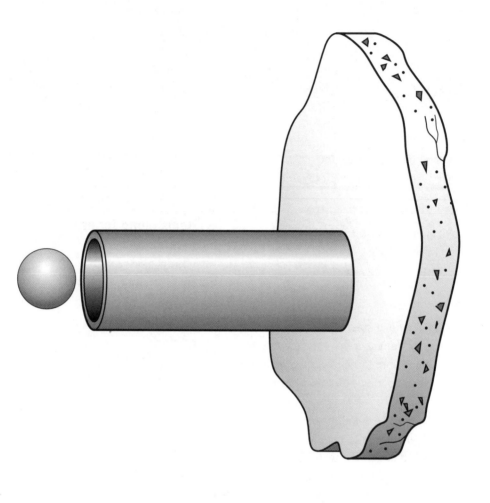

1 large shifter
1 plastic shower screen
1 carpenter's saw
1 tennis ball
1 ball of string
2 rolls of toilet paper
1 small jar of honey
1 unopened bottle of wine
2 sheets of writing paper
2 ceramic cups
2 pens
4 unused party balloons
1 pair of reading glasses
2 raw eggs
1 unopened can of soft drink
1 small chili plant

20

Alphabet Soup # 1

ITM

TIME REQUIRED	SIZE OF GROUP	MATERIAL REQUIRED
5 minutes.	Unlimited.	None.

Overview

It seems as if trainers are always after ways of breaking large groups down into smaller groups. This is one way of sorting participants out.

Goals

1. To break down a large group into smaller groups with a random mix.
2. To get participants moving.

Procedure

1. Inform the group that they are going to break up into smaller groups for the next activity.
2. What you now require them to do is to form a straight line. The person at one end of the line will have their middle name starting with the letter closest to A while the person at the other end will have their middle name starting with the letter closest to Z.
3. Before they begin to form their line, tell them that the exercise must be conducted on a non-verbal basis!
4. After the line has been formed you or the participants may like to check their accuracy.

5. With the line formed the facilitator can now divide it into the right number of groups required.

Discussion point

1. How did they arrive at their correct positions?

Variations

1. May be conducted without the non-verbal rule.
2. May be conducted as a verbal exercise but with their eyes closed or blindfolds on.

TRAINER'S NOTES

21

Population

ITCFMXL

TIME REQUIRED	SIZE OF GROUP	MATERIAL REQUIRED
40–60 minutes.	Unlimited.	Sufficient copies of the 'Population Sheet'.

Overview

This activity has been designed to show how teamwork can improve the end result.

Goals

1. To allow participants a chance to see synergy and its benefits in operation.
2. To encourage interaction among participants.

Procedure

1. Introduce the exercise and hand out a copy of the 'Population Sheet' to each participant. Ask them to complete the sheet in 5 minutes without any discussion.
2. When the individuals have completed the sheet, get them to form groups of 5–7 participants. Tell groups they have 15 minutes to reach a consensus on the correct answers.
3. After the groups have reached a consensus, lead a discussion into improved decision making, synergy and so on. A sample chart around which to base the discussion can be found on page 53.

Discussion points

1. Why were the group scores generally better than any individual score?
2. How was the leadership exercised in the group?
3. How well was time utilised?

Variations

1. After the groups have completed the consensus-building phase, another phase can be added where all subgroups now have to reach a consensus that represents the whole group of participants.
2. Use countries, states or any set of data the participants may have some familiarity with (see examples below).

Solutions

Australian locations:

Sydney, NSW	3,770,100
Melbourne, VIC	3,217,400
Brisbane, QLD	1,488,900
Perth, WA	1,262,200
Adelaide, SA	1,080,700
Newcastle, NSW	465,900
Canberra, ACT	332,100
Gold Coast, QLD	319,100
Wollongong, NSW	253,600
Hobart, TAS	194,800
Geelong, VIC	152,700
Darwin, NT	79,200

Countries:

China	1,236,910,000
USA	270,310,000
India	984,000,000
Indonesia	212,940,000
Japan	125,930,000
Germany	82,080,000
Thailand	60,040,000
UK	58,970,000
Malaysia	20,930,000
Australia	18,750,000
Hong Kong	6,710,000
Papua New Guinea	4,600,000
New Zealand	3,630,000
Singapore	3,490,000

Australian states:

New South Wales	5,544,000
Victoria	4,165,000
Queensland	3,593,000
Western Australia	1,441,000
South Australia	1,373,000
Tasmania	447,000
Australian Capital Territory	264,000
Northern Territory	148,000

Distribution of the workforce in Australia:

Wholesale and Retail Trade	1,796,500
Health and Community Services	817,900
Manufacturing	1,084,000
Finance, Property & Business Services	1,272,000
Accommodation, Cafés and Restaurants	411,500
Construction	644,200
Recreation, Personal & Other Services	560,700
Agriculture	418,800
Transport and Storage	402,800
Mining	82,100

Figures accurate as of January, 1999.

(**Source:** Australian Bureau of Statistics.)

TRAINER'S NOTES

Figures and places will have to be altered or rewritten for different countries.

Population Sheet

Rearrange these locations in order of population size.

Adelaide, SA
Brisbane, QLD
Canberra, ACT
Darwin, NT
Geelong, VIC
Gold Coast, QLD
Hobart, TAS
Melbourne, VIC
Newcastle, NSW
Perth, WA
Sydney, NSW
Wollongong, NSW

Population (Group Discussion Sheet)

	Group	Group	Group	Group
1. Group score				
2. Average individual score				
3. Difference between 1 and 2				
4. Best individual score				
5. Difference between 1 and 4				
6. Worst individual score				
7. Difference between 1 and 6				

123 Go

TIME REQUIRED	SIZE OF GROUP	MATERIAL REQUIRED
2–5 minutes.	Unlimited.	None.

Overview

This exercise demonstrates how visual signals are as significant as verbal signals.

Goal

1. To allow participants to see how people react to non-verbal communication.

Procedure

1. Tell the group that they are going to be asked to clap their hands on the count of 'three'.
2. Count out loudly 'one' (pause), 'two' (pause) and then clap your own hands **before** the count of 'three'. Some of the group members will follow what they see and clap their hands as well. Then call out 'three' and the rest of the group will clap their hands.

3. A discussion can now be led into the importance of matching verbal and non-verbal signals. If your audience are trainers, the discussion may be led into the value and importance of appropriate visual aids.

Discussion points

1. How many people clapped their hands before the count of 'three'? Why?
2. How would this exercise work with everyone's eyes closed?
3. How does this apply in the workplace?
4. What does this exercise let trainers/presenters know?

Variation

1. Any other visual action may be substituted.

TRAINER'S NOTES

23

More Whispers

ITCMLS

TIME REQUIRED	SIZE OF GROUP	MATERIAL REQUIRED
10–15 minutes, depending on group size.	Unlimited, but needs to be broken into subgroups of 6–10.	A copy of 'The Message' for the facilitator.

Overview

This popular activity has been reworked again to show how messages may get distorted.

Goals

1. To allow participants to see how messages may get mixed up.
2. To identify ways of improving communication.

Procedure

1. Select one participant and quietly read 'The Message' to them, making sure no one else can hear.
2. This person is now to whisper the message on to the person sitting next to them.
3. They in turn pass the message on to the person sitting next to them and so on until the last person is given the message.
4. This person is now to tell everyone what the final message was.
5. After the laughter, the facilitator reads aloud the initial message.
6. Discussion should now follow into ways of improving communication and why communication breaks down.

Discussion points

1. Why did the message break down?
2. Do people sometimes sabotage communications? Why?
3. How could we improve this process?
4. How does this relate to everyday activities?

Variations

1. Individuals may pass their message on to each other outside the room.
2. With large groups you may elect to form small groups of 6–10 participants and take one person from each group as the starter.

'The Message'

I was just talking to a person who saw a hold-up this morning. They told me that they had witnessed a bank being held up at 10:15 this morning at [City/Suburb]. Three people went into the bank with automatic revolvers. Two had balaclavas on and one had a mask of Donald Duck.

TRAINER'S NOTES

Under no circumstances should your copy of 'The Message' be given to anyone during the activity.

24

Uniqueness

IT

TIME REQUIRED	SIZE OF GROUP	MATERIAL REQUIRED
5 minutes.	Unlimited.	A sheet of paper and pen for each participant.

Overview

An activity designed to encourage some self-disclosure.

Goal

1. To allow participants to share some information about themselves with the rest of the group.

Procedure

1. Give each person a sheet of paper and a pen.
2. Ask them to write down one thing that they believe is unique about themselves. Examples may include things like writing poetry, having met a movie star, collecting paintings, writing books and so on.
3. After everyone has written something down, all of the sheets should be collected and shuffled.
4. Sheets are now read out one at a time and participants try to guess whose unique characteristic it is. Points can be awarded for each correct guess. The person with the highest score at the end may be awarded a prize.

Discussion points

1. Was it easy to guess who each sheet belonged to?
2. What made it easy/hard? Lead into a discussion about stereotypes and expectations.

Variation

1. If you have an extremely large group, smaller groups could be formed.

TRAINER'S NOTES

Age Split

ITM

TIME REQUIRED	SIZE OF GROUP	MATERIAL REQUIRED
5 minutes.	Unlimited.	None.

Overview

This is another way of breaking a large group down into smaller groups.

Goals

1. To break a large group into smaller groups with a random mix.
2. To get participants moving.

Procedure

1. Inform the group that they are going to break up into smaller groups for the next activity.
2. What you now require them to do is to form a straight line with the youngest person at one end and the person with the most life experience at the other end. The one rule for this activity is that it has to be done in complete silence.
3. After the line has been formed you or the participants may like to check their accuracy.
4. With the line formed the facilitator can now divide it into the right number of groups required.

Discussion point

1. Did everybody find their correct position?

Variations

1. May be conducted without the non-verbal rule.
2. May be conducted with eyes closed or blindfolds on.

TRAINER'S NOTES

26

Break Up

ITM

TIME REQUIRED	SIZE OF GROUP	MATERIAL REQUIRED
1 minute.	Unlimited.	None.

Overview

This activity is a way to divide a group into two.

Goal

1. To break a large group into two smaller groups.

Procedure

1. Inform the group that they are going to form two smaller groups.
2. Using certain criteria ask the group to break into two smaller groups. Participants can be asked to form groups according to eye colour, shoe colour, whether or not they wear glasses and so on.

Discussion points

None.

Variations

1. Make the division based on the month in which people are born (e.g. January–June, July–December).
2. Select other criteria through observation.

TRAINER'S NOTES

You must make certain observations before conducting this activity.

27

Colour Split

ITM

TIME REQUIRED	SIZE OF GROUP	MATERIAL REQUIRED
1 minute.	Unlimited.	Prepared name tag for each participant.

Overview

Yet another way to form small groups randomly.

Goal

1. To break a large group into smaller groups with a random mix.

Procedure

1. Inform the group that they are going to be broken into smaller groups.
2. Ask the participants to look at their name tags and find a coloured spot in the corner (or on the back etc.).
3. They should now find other people with spots the same colour and form their new groups.

Discussion points

None.

Variations

1. Use letters or numbers instead of colours.
2. Write the participants' names in colour rather than using coloured spots.
3. Use different coloured backing sheets or other symbols instead of coloured spots.

TRAINER'S NOTES

28

Jigsaw Sort

ITM

TIME REQUIRED	SIZE OF GROUP	MATERIAL REQUIRED
5 minutes.	Unlimited.	A small jigsaw puzzle for each subgroup. Each puzzle should contain the same number of pieces as the group has members.

Overview

Another activity to facilitate random sorting of participants into groups.

Goal

1. To break a large group into smaller groups with a random mix.

Procedure

1. Advise the group that they are going to participate in an activity. Ask participants to look in their folder (under their chair etc.) and locate a single piece of a jigsaw puzzle.
2. Ask them to mix with everyone to find parts that fit with their piece.
3. After all puzzles have been completed tell participants that they are now with the other members of their new group.

Discussion points

None.

Variations

1. Use a large jigsaw puzzle and select small areas for each group. The areas should not have common sides.
2. Use magazine/newspaper pages torn into the correct number of pieces.

TRAINER'S NOTES

29

Morning Tea Cake

MX

TIME REQUIRED	SIZE OF GROUP	MATERIAL REQUIRED
No extra time required.	Unlimited, but needs to be broken into subgroups of 5–7 people.	At least one cake for each subgroup.

Overview

A problem-solving activity for participants to solve before they can eat their cake supplied for the coffee break.

Goals

1. To have participants participate in a simple problem-solving activity.
2. To encourage communication among participants.

Procedure

1. Inform the participants that it is now time for their coffee break.
2. However, due to lack of resources, each group only has one cake. Tell them that, to test their problem-solving abilities, they will have to cut their own cakes. The problem is that they are allowed to make no more than three cuts to divide the cake.

3. After the cake has been cut into the correct number of pieces, they may now proceed with their coffee break.

Discussion points

1. Did everyone get some cake?
2. Did the group come up with a realistic solution? Why? Why not?

Variations

1. Use a different number of cuts.
2. Get participants to complete the activity non-verbally.

Solutions

See following page.

TRAINER'S NOTES

Spare cakes for the coffee break may be required as some may be completely destroyed during the activity.

Morning Tea Cake—Possible Cuts

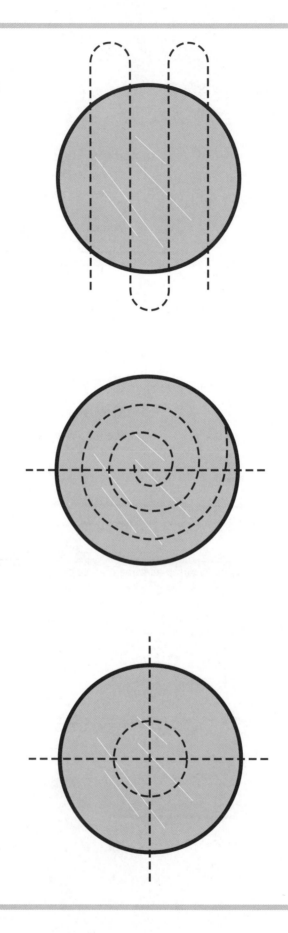

30

Who's With Whom?

ITCMX

TIME REQUIRED	SIZE OF GROUP	MATERIAL REQUIRED
5–10 minutes.	Unlimited, but a minimum of 18–20.	None.

Overview

An activity designed to look at a problem-solving process and to start groups working together.

Goals

1. To allow a large group to break into smaller groups.
2. To allow participants to become involved in a problem-solving activity.
3. To encourage interaction.
4. To get participants moving.

Procedure

1. Tell the group that they are going to become involved in a problem-solving activity. Add that for the activity to work properly, they will need to form small groups of 5–7 people. Give them 1 minute to form their groups.
2. After groups have been formed, tell them that the problem-solving activity has now been completed.

The problem was for them to form smaller groups.

3. A discussion can now be led in the desired area/s.

Discussion points

1. How long did it take?
2. How were the groups formed? Was it effective? Why? Why not?
3. Did people take on certain roles?
4. How does this relate to the workplace?

Variations

1. Get them to form smaller groups (i.e. 3–4 people).
2. Get them to conduct the activity non-verbally.
3. If this activity is used at the beginning of a program, the individuals in the newly formed groups may also be required to introduce themselves to the rest of their team before the program starts.

TRAINER'S NOTES

31

Finished Early

CFMXE

TIME REQUIRED	SIZE OF GROUP	MATERIAL REQUIRED
No set time.	Unlimited, but should be split into small groups of 5–7 people.	None.

Overview

An exercise to use for the profitable employment of any time that may be left at the end of a session or program.

Goals

1. To make productive use of left-over time.
2. To resolve any outstanding questions or issues.

Procedure

1. At the end of a session or program, if you find you have time left over get the group to form smaller groups of 5–7 people. As groups, they should formulate three questions for the facilitator (you) to answer.

2. Set an appropriate time limit for groups to form their questions.
3. At the end of this time ask each group for their questions and either answer them right away or display them for group discussion.

Discussion point

1. Did group members tend to answer questions as they were raised?

Variations

1. Individuals may be asked to come up with one question each relating to any outstanding issues.
2. Get participants to answer the questions themselves if possible.

TRAINER'S NOTES

There will generally be a number of outstanding questions, but in many cases the participant may not have been listening or may have been distracted at the time. Questions raised by individuals are often answered by the other group members.

32

Impressions

ITCMPS

TIME REQUIRED	SIZE OF GROUP	MATERIAL REQUIRED
30–60 minutes.	Unlimited, but not so large that the facilitator cannot eavesdrop on the conversations with ease.	A prepared overhead transparency or flip-chart with the questions displayed.

Overview

An activity to get participants to disclose the first impressions they had of each other.

Goals

1. To allow participants the opportunity to disclose their first impressions of each other.
2. To improve communication among participants.
3. To break down some of the barriers that may be in place.
4. To develop more trust among participants.

Procedure

1. Ask the group to think back to the time they first met each other.
2. Get them to form pairs to reveal those first thoughts. Only now should you show them the prepared questions. Allow enough time for participants to discuss all of the questions.

Discussion points

1. Are all of our first impressions accurate?
2. Should we rely solely on first impressions?
3. Were these first impressions fair? Why? Why not?

Variations

1. Groups of 3 or 4 may be used instead of pairs.
2. The questions can be prepared as handouts.
3. Put all participants' names into a hat and draw out pairs or groups.

First Impressions

1. What was your first impression of me?
2. Why did you have that impression?
3. Who did I remind you of? Why?
4. How accurate do you now think that first impression was?

TRAINER'S NOTES

Emphasise to participants that this activity is to be treated constructively, not destructively.

First Impressions

1. What was your first impression of me?

2. Why did you have that impression?

3. Who did I remind you of? Why?

4. How accurate do you now think that first impression was?

33

Rope Circles

ITCMXPES

TIME REQUIRED	SIZE OF GROUP	MATERIAL REQUIRED
15–30 minutes plus discussion time.	Unlimited, but larger groups may need to be broken into smaller groups of 10 to 12 people.	A rope for each group, about 2.5 metres per participant. A blindfold will also be required for each person.

Overview

An activity with a difference designed to improve communications, problem solving and so on.

Goals

1. To show ways of improving communications within a group.
2. To allow participants to participate in a problem-solving activity.
3. To get the group moving.

Procedure

1. Advise the group that they are going to participate in an unusual problem-solving activity. The whole activity should be described before participants are required to put their blindfolds in place.
2. Tell participants that, after they have their blindfolds on, a bag will be placed in front of them containing a length of rope.
3. Their task is to get the rope out of the bag and form a circle with each of them hanging on to the rope, in such a way that they are equally spaced around the circle.

4. After the activity has been completed, lead the discussion into ways of improving communications or improving the decision-making process. It may also be useful to discuss the different roles people took on and any assumptions they made about the activity.

Discussion points

1. How successful was the group in forming the circle? What contributed to this success or lack of it?
2. What roles did people take on?
3. What made it easy?
4. What made it hard?
5. What would improve the result?
6. What assumptions did people make? (E.g. did the entire rope need to be used?)
7. How does this activity relate to the workplace?

Variations

1. May be conducted non-verbally for well-established groups.
2. You may wish to identify observers for this activity.
3. May be conducted a second time to see if results improve.

TRAINER'S NOTES

Blindfolds can often be obtained from large hotels/motels/airlines/railways and so on. People should be given the opportunity to not participate in this activity or to withdraw from it if they wish. These people may like to observe.

34

Rope Squares

ITCMXPES

TIME REQUIRED	SIZE OF GROUP	MATERIAL REQUIRED
15–30 minutes plus discussion time.	Unlimited, but larger groups may need to be broken into smaller groups of 10 to 12 people.	A rope for each group, about 2.5 metres per participant. A blindfold will also be required for each person.

Overview

Another unusual activity designed to improve communications and problem-solving abilities.

Goals

1. To show ways of improving communications within a group.
2. To get participants involved in a problem-solving activity.
3. To look at assumptions people make.
4. To get the group moving.

Procedure

1. Advise the group that they are going to participate in an unusual problem-solving activity. The whole activity should be described before participants are required to put their blindfolds in place.
2. Tell participants that, after they have their blindfolds on, a bag will be placed in front of them containing a length of rope.
3. Their task is to get the rope out of the bag and form a square with each of them holding on to the rope, in such a way that they are equally spaced around the square.
4. After the activity has been completed, lead the discussion into ways of improving

communications or improving the decision-making process. It may also be useful to discuss the different roles people took on and any assumptions they made about the activity.

Discussion points

1. How successful was the group in forming the square? What contributed to this success or lack of it?
2. What roles did people take on?
3. What made it easy?
4. What made it hard?
5. What would improve the result?
6. What assumptions did people make? (E.g. did the entire rope need to be used?)
7. How does this activity relate to the workplace?

Variations

1. May be conducted non-verbally for well-established groups.
2. You may wish to identify observers for this activity.
3. May be conducted a second time to see if results improve.
4. Put a few knots in the rope before the activity commences. People sometimes incorrectly assume that these are corners.

TRAINER'S NOTES

Blindfolds can often be obtained from large hotels/motels/airlines/railways and so on. People should be given the opportunity to not participate in this activity or to withdraw from it if they wish. These people may like to observe.

35

Assumptions

TIME REQUIRED	SIZE OF GROUP	MATERIAL REQUIRED
No extra time required.	Unlimited.	Whiteboard and marker or flip-chart and marker.

Overview

A quick activity to show that people should not make too many assumptions.

Goal

1. To show participants in a light-hearted way why they should not make too many assumptions.

Procedure

1. During group discussions, if you overhear people making assumptions about certain things you can write the word 'assume' on the whiteboard or flip-chart.
2. Call for quiet and asked the group if they know why the word 'assume' is spelt the way it is.
3. When there are no responses, draw two vertical lines between the letters 's' and 'u', and 'u' and 'm'.
4. The group can now see that the word 'assume' forms three separate words. You can tell them that if you assume too much you will make an 'ass' of 'u' and 'me'.

Discussion points

None.

Variations

None.

TRAINER'S NOTES

36
The Debate

ICMLE

TIME REQUIRED	SIZE OF GROUP	MATERIAL REQUIRED
Variable, but preferably over a period of days or weeks.	Unlimited, but the activity will need to be modified for different sizes of groups.	None.

Overview

An activity to get the group involved in locating information about a certain topic.

Goals

1. To encourage participants to locate relevant sources of information.
2. To encourage self-directed learning.
3. To get a group working together.

Procedure

1. Advise the group that they will need to break into an even number of smaller groups for this activity. Groups of three are best.
2. After the groups have been formed, groups should pair off for a debate. One group from each pair will be responsible for presenting the case for the motion while the other group will be responsible for presenting the case against it.
3. Now give the pairs of groups their topics; one pair will be for and one against the motion. Note: All topics must be relevant to the program and to the group's needs. At this stage you should allot a period of time for research and preparation. Ideally, the groups would be required to present their case in several days' or weeks' time.
4. After the cases have been prepared, a debate is conducted with the balance of participants voting on the motion. After the first pair of groups is heard and voted on, a discussion should follow. After the discussion, next pair of groups should be heard and so on until all debates are concluded.

Discussion points

1. As appropriate to the topics chosen.

Variations

1. May be done individually if the group is small (i.e. one person for and one against each motion).
2. If presentation skills are part of the program, participants should be encouraged to use appropriate presentation aids.

TRAINER'S NOTES

Do you wish to impose any rules on the debate?

37

Introductions

ITL

TIME REQUIRED	SIZE OF GROUP	MATERIAL REQUIRED
Depends on numbers.	Unlimited, but for very large groups it may be advisable to form smaller ones.	A whiteboard and marker or a sheet of flip-chart paper or a prepared overhead transparency.

Overview

This activity allows participants to introduce themselves to the whole group in a non-threatening way.

Goals

1. To have each person introduce themselves to the group.
2. To encourage interaction among the group members outside the training environment.

Procedure

1. After the facilitator introduces the course and him/herself, the participants are asked to introduce themselves.
2. A prepared overhead transparency (whiteboard or flip-chart) is displayed to show what is to be

mentioned during the introductions. The facilitator may wish to use this method to introduce him/herself.

- Who am I?
- Where do I come from? Place/company/job etc.
- Why am I here?
- What do I want from this course?
- What is one unusual thing about myself?

Discussion points

None.

Variation

1. The topic areas may be altered to suit the group.

TRAINER'S NOTES

You will normally find that the 'unusual' disclosure is the starting point for many conversations during the breaks.

Introductions

- Who am I?

- Where do I come from? Place/company/job etc.

- Why am I here?

- What do I want from this course?

- What is one unusual thing about myself?

38

Taped In

TCMX

TIME REQUIRED	SIZE OF GROUP	MATERIAL REQUIRED
5–10 minutes.	Unlimited.	One roll of coloured adhesive, masking or packing tape.

Overview

A lively activity designed to get the participants working together while having fun.

Goals

1. To get participants working together.
2. To build team spirit.
3. To have participants become involved in an enjoyable problem-solving activity.
4. To get everyone moving.

Procedure

1. Before the group arrive, mark out a square on the floor according to the principle set out in the Trainer's notes below.
2. Advise the group that they are going to become involved in a problem-solving activity.
3. Their task is to get as many people as possible inside the square and not touching the tape. Allow a couple of minutes for discussion and trial attempts.
4. After the final attempt has been made, the facilitator should lead a discussion on teamwork, improved communications etc.

Discussion points

1. How many people did you get into the square?
2. What helped the final result?

3. What hindered the final result?
4. How many could you get in if you were allowed another attempt? (Do you want to try?)

Variations

1. Inform the group that they will only be given one attempt. All planning must be completed before the attempt in the square.
2. Use a sheet of flip-chart paper instead of the taped square. Be careful as this can be very slippery on carpet.

TRAINER'S NOTES

The taped square should be fixed to the floor before training commences. The size of the square is important. Try to estimate the smallest square possible for the group—and then halve it!

39
Multiplication

XLPE

TIME REQUIRED	SIZE OF GROUP	MATERIAL REQUIRED
5 minutes.	Unlimited.	None, but a prepared overhead of the results will make it easier.

Overview

A quick activity designed to show participants how some snap decisions may not be the best.

Goals

1. To have participants participate in a quick decision-making activity.
2. To demonstrate how important it is sometimes to spend a little more time making decisions.

Procedure

1. Advise the participants that they are going to be offered a job that will take one month (31 days) to complete. If they take the job they have a choice of how they will be remunerated.
2. Explain the two choices available. They can elect to be paid $10,000 per day for each day they work or they can be paid 1¢ for the first day and have their pay doubled every day until the job is completed.
3. Quickly take a vote on which method people would choose.
4. The majority (if not all) will choose the $10,000-a-day option. You can now advise them that if

they had chosen the other option the outcome would have been as follows.

> $10,000 a day
> > After 31 days = $310,000.00
> $0.01 on first day then double every day after that
> > After 31 days = $21,474,836.47

Discussion points

1. How many people selected the most rewarding way?
2. Why do most people select the $10,000-a-day option?
3. How does this relate to the workplace?

Variation

1. May be conducted individually initially but, before the solution is shown, small groups may be formed to come up with a group answer. This will generally lead to the more profitable solution being selected.

TRAINER'S NOTES

Multiplication

$10,000 a day

   After 31 days = $310,000.00

$0.01 on first day then double every day after that

   After 31 days = $21,474,836.47

40

Additions

ICFMXLPE

TIME REQUIRED
2–5 minutes.

SIZE OF GROUP
Unlimited.

MATERIAL REQUIRED
None necessary but a prepared overhead transparency may be used to reveal the numbers in the desired sequence.

Overview

A quick activity to demonstrate to participants how important it is to sequence information correctly.

Goals

1. To allow participants to participate in an activity that demonstrates the importance of sequencing information.
2. To highlight the fact that the trainer is just as responsible as the learner for correct learning to take place.

Procedure

1. Inform the participants that they are going to be involved in an activity requiring them to add several numbers together. Add that they are required to call out the correct answers as they go through the sums.
2. The group should be given the first two numbers (1000 and 40). As they say the total ask them to call out louder as you are finding it difficult to hear them. Continue giving one number at a time encouraging them to call out the answers. The numbers and the sequence are as follows. 1000, 40, 1000, 30, 1000, 20, 1000, 10.
3. As the group call out 5000 as their final answer, thank them. Now ask them to add exactly the same numbers but in a different sequence. The numbers are now given using the same techniques but in the following order. 10, 20, 30, 40, 1000, 1000, 1000, 1000.
4. After the group give you the answer of 4100, you can now ask them why they arrived at a different answer using exactly the same numbers. Lead the discussion into the importance of giving information in the correct sequence.

Discussion points

1. Why are the two answers different?
2. Why is the sequence important?
3. Whose responsibility is it to ensure information is correctly understood?

Variations

None.

TRAINER'S NOTES

41

Notepads

TIME REQUIRED	SIZE OF GROUP	MATERIAL REQUIRED
90–120 minutes.	Unlimited, but large groups will have to be broken down into smaller groups of 5–7 people.	Each group will require a copy of the 'Notepad Instructions Sheet', 'Finance Sheet' and 'Order Form'. Each may need 2 staplers, 3 rulers, 3 pairs of scissors, a ream of A4 paper (used paper is okay), a ream of A5 paper (used paper is okay), a number of A4 coloured sheets (to be used as covers) and a roll of binding tape.

Overview

An interesting and fun activity designed to demonstrate to groups the value of planning.

Goals

1. To demonstrate to participants the value of planning.
2. To improve communication among participants.
3. To get participants moving.
4. To have fun!

Procedure

1. Split the group into smaller groups of 5–7 people. Advise groups that they will be participating in an exercise in which they will be required to produce notepads to a set standard. They will need to come up with some costings and then prepare an order form to purchase the raw materials from you.
2. Give each group a copy of the 'Notepad Instructions Sheet', 'Finance Sheet' and 'Order Form'.

3. They now have 60 minutes to complete the activity.
4. At the end of the activity each group will assess their own performance based on two criteria:
   - the number of notepads made to specification within a 60-minute period
   - the number of notepads **actually** made against the number **planned**.

Discussion points

1. Which group had the greatest profit (or perhaps the least loss)?
2. What assisted each group?
3. What hindered each group?
4. Would more planning time have been of use?
5. How does this relate to the workplace?

Variations

1. The time frame may be altered.
2. Larger groups may be used.

TRAINER'S NOTES

You may like to make a cardboard template to check the dimensions of the finished notepads. This will make it much easier to check the completed products. The template should be the exact size and also show the exact location of the staples. It will then just be a matter of seeing whether the finished products are within the ±3 mm tolerance.

Notepad Instruction Sheet

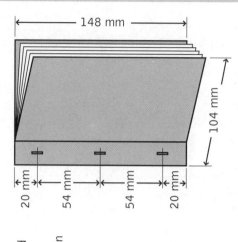

The activity

In your teams, you are to make notepads to a set standard using the materials provided. At the end of the activity, each group will assess their performance according to the following criteria:

- the number of notepads made to specification within a 60-minute period, and
- the number of notepads **actually** made against the number **planned**.

The forms

Material costs

On hire for 60 minutes:

- Staplers (maximum of 2 per team) $50.00 each
- Scissors (maximum of 3 per team) $20.00 each
- Rulers (maximum of 3 per team) $15.00 each

To purchase:

- Cover sheet material A4 size $8.00 per sheet
- Paper A4 size $2.00 per sheet
- Paper A5 size $4.00 per sheet
- Binding tape $4.00 per 300 mm

Labour costs

Labour costs are $2.00 for each person-minute during production.

Contracts

The following contract is offered for the purchase of the notepads you produce in the 60 minutes.

- All notepads must adhere to set standards.
- All dimensions for the notepads must be within 3 mm of stated specifications.

- All notepads meeting standards will be bought for $40.00 each. As part of the tender, each company must state beforehand, how many notepads they could produce.
- Any notepads produced in excess of the estimate will be bought at $5.00 each.
- Any shortfall in notepads produced below the amount contracted will incur a $30.00 fee per pad.

Notepad standards

The finished notepad has 24 pages (12 leaves) and coloured front and back covers. Three staples through both covers and the pages hold the notepad together. The spine is covered by a 25 mm tape backing strip.

Quality specifications

- All dimensions are ±3 mm.
- All open edges of the notepad to be clean cut.
- Staples must be well turned in and covered on both sides.
- Staples must not protrude through the tape.
- Tape must be smoothed down firmly all over.
- Corners must be square and sides parallel.

Finance Sheet

Costs

Equipment	Staplers		
	Scissors		
	Rulers		
Materials	Cover sheets		
	Paper A4		
	Paper A5		
	Tape		
Labour	Person-minutes		
	Total costs		

Sales

	Total sales	

Profit/Loss

	Total sales	
	Total costs	
	Net profit/loss	

Order Form

Company Name:

Please supply us with the following items:

Item	Quantity	Cost	Total
Staplers		$50.00 each	
Scissors		$20.00 each	
Rulers		$15.00 each	
Cover sheets		$8.00 each sheet	
Sheets A4 paper		$2.00 each sheet	
Sheets A5 paper		$4.00 each sheet	
Tape		$4.00 each 300 mm	

We aim to make _____ notepads within
60 minutes and understand the fee for short deliveries.

Signed: _____ (for the group)

42

Mix Up

ITM

TIME REQUIRED	SIZE OF GROUP	MATERIAL REQUIRED
5 minutes.	Unlimited, but with a minimum of around 12.	None.

Overview

An activity designed to get the group on their feet and have a little fun.

Goals

1. To get participants moving.
2. To liven things up.

Procedure

1. Ask each participant to select two other people in the group (without telling them) and identify them as 'A' and 'B'.
2. Now ask the group to stand up and get as close as possible to the person they selected as their 'A'. At the same time they are to keep as far away from their 'B' as they possibly can.
3. Sit back and watch the fun and activity.

Discussion point

1. Did that get the circulation going?

Variation

1. The facilitator may participate.

TRAINER'S NOTES

43

What Is It?

ICMXP

TIME REQUIRED	SIZE OF GROUP	MATERIAL REQUIRED
10–20 minutes.	Unlimited, but needs to be broken up into subgroups of 5–7 participants.	A prepared overhead transparency or flip-chart sheet. A sheet of paper and a pen for each group.

Overview

An activity to get people working together in small groups.

Goals

1. To allow participants to become involved in a problem-solving activity.
2. To encourage interaction among participants.
3. To look at the effects of synergy.
4. To get participants moving.

Procedure

1. Advise the group that they are going to become involved in a problem-solving activity.
2. The large group is to break into smaller groups of 5–7 people.
3. After the groups have been formed, show them the prepared diagram and ask them to find as many answers as they can to the question, 'What is it?' Five minutes should be allowed.
4. When the five minutes are up, call for the groups' completed lists. Their answers may be listed beside the diagram.

5. After all ideas have been listed, the entire group can be told that there isn't a correct answer. The purpose of the activity was to show the effect of synergy, which should now be used for the rest of the course and/or back in the workplace.

Discussion points

1. What is it?
2. Were all of the answers realistic?
3. How can this activity link with the rest of the course or back to the workplace?

Variations

1. May be done individually rather than in small groups.
2. May be done individually at first, after which groups form to share ideas and to develop more.
3. A different picture could be used.

TRAINER'S NOTES

The picture is of an hourglass.

What Is It?

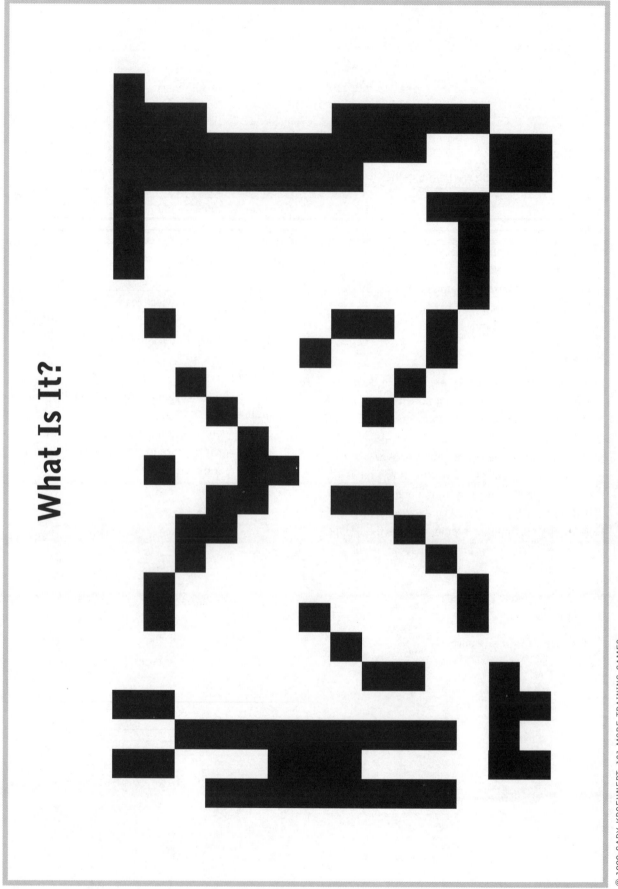

44

The Circle and the Dot

ITMXP

TIME REQUIRED	SIZE OF GROUP	MATERIAL REQUIRED
2 minutes.	Unlimited.	A whiteboard and marker or a sheet of flip-chart paper and marker or a prepared overhead transparency. Each person will also require a sheet of paper and a pen.

Overview

A problem-solving activity to get individuals to employ lateral thinking, that is, to think beyond customary self-imposed boundaries.

Goals

1. To allow participants to become involved in a problem-solving activity.
2. To encourage participants to think beyond customary self-imposed boundaries.

Procedure

1. Draw or show the circle-and-dot diagram and ask participants to think of as many ways as possible of reproducing the diagram without taking their pen off the paper. Allow 60 seconds.
2. After asking people to stop, call for solutions to the problem.

3. After all ideas have been heard, you may want to suggest some other ways.
4. Lead the discussion into the topics of lateral thinking and assumptions or something more directly relevant to the group's needs.

Discussion points

1. How many ways did people find?
2. What limited our thinking or problem-solving abilities?
3. Is it always relevant to find more than one solution? Why? Why not?

Variation

1. May be conducted in small groups.

TRAINER'S NOTES

Some ways of reproducing the circle and the dot: folding; taking the paper off the pen rather than vice versa; photocopying the original; using a still camera, video camera, scanner.

The Circle and the Dot

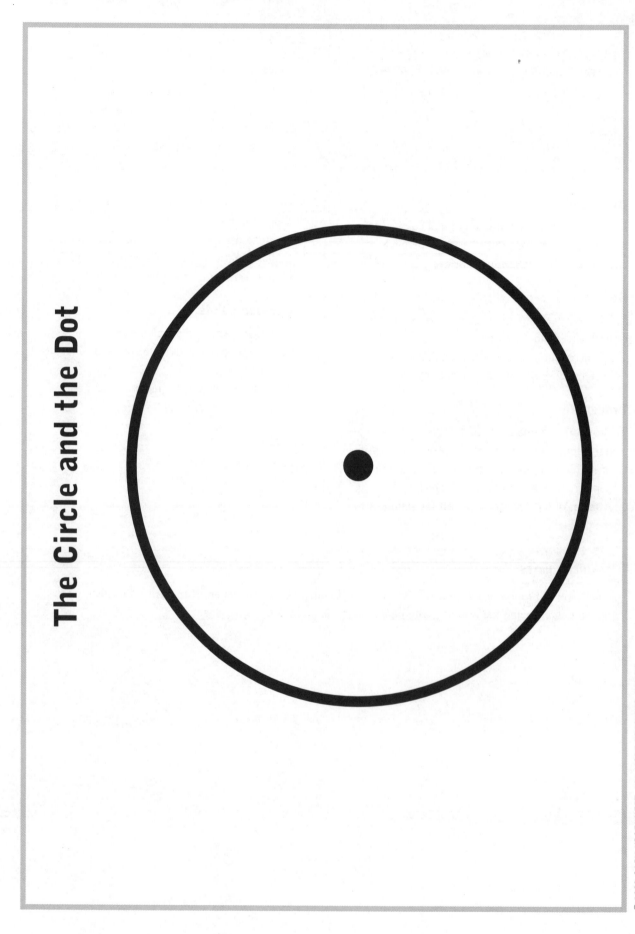

45

Magazine Mix Up

ITCMXLP

TIME REQUIRED	SIZE OF GROUP	MATERIAL REQUIRED
20–30 minutes.	Unlimited, but needs to be broken into subgroups of 5–7.	One magazine for each group. Magazines need to have all of the separate pages torn out and the page numbers removed.

Overview

An activity designed to get individuals in small groups working together.

Goals

1. To encourage interaction among participants.
2. To encourage participants to communicate.
3. To allow people to participate in a problem-solving activity in a small group.

Procedure

1. Divide the group into smaller groups of 5–7 participants and advise them that they will be participating in a problem-solving activity.
2. Now give each group their prepared magazine. Their task is to put the magazine together in the correct page sequence.
3. After all groups have finished check to make sure they have the correct sequence of pages.
4. When all groups have completed the activity lead a discussion into appropriate topic areas, for example, team building, communications, perceptions, decision making, problem solving and so on.

Discussion points

1. Was the sequence correct?
2. What helped the group in arriving at its final decision?
3. What hindered the group in arriving at its final decision?
4. How does this activity relate to the workplace?

Variations

1. Use magazines in different languages.
2. Use more than one magazine per group, but all of similar format and of the same size.
3. May be conducted as a competitive exercise.

TRAINER'S NOTES

You may require two copies of each magazine: one for the exercise and to show them (or prove) the correct sequence.

46

Magazine Messages

TCMXL

TIME REQUIRED	SIZE OF GROUP	MATERIAL REQUIRED
40–60 minutes.	Unlimited, but needs to broken into subgroups of 5–7.	Each group requires one magazine, which must have all of the separate pages torn out and the page numbers removed. Each magazine should have a secret message written with lemon juice over several pages. One box of matches or a lighter for each group.

Overview

This activity is based on 'Magazine Mix Up' but contains an additional problem for participants to solve.

Goals

1. To encourage interaction between participants.
2. To encourage participants to communicate.
3. To allow people to participate in a small group problem-solving activity.

Procedure

1. Divide the group into smaller groups of 5–7 participants and advise them that they will be participating in a problem-solving activity.
2. Now give each group their prepared magazine. Their task is to put the magazine together in the correct page sequence.
3. After all groups have finished check to make sure they have the correct sequence of pages.
4. When all groups have completed the activity lead a discussion into appropriate topic areas, for example, team building, communications, perceptions, decision making, problem solving and so on.

5. Now tell each group that their magazine contains a secret message. The message is located in sequence at the top of the pages. The message is written in lemon juice so they will need to use their matches to find it.

Note: To read the secret message a flame must be held under the page to darken the lemon juice.

Discussion points

1. What was the secret message?
2. What helped the group in arriving at its final decision?
3. What hindered the group in arriving at its final decision?
4. How does this activity relate to the workplace?

Variations

1. Use magazines in different languages.
2. Use more than one magazine per group, but all of similar format and of the same size.
3. May be conducted as a competitive exercise.
4. This activity works very well if a photocopy of a lengthy report/document/manual is used (say 30–40 pages) instead of a magazine.
5. Messages can be anything at all.

TRAINER'S NOTES

1. There are obvious safety issues.
2. Choose appropriate messages, such as 'It's coffee time!'

47

What Am I?

ICMX

TIME REQUIRED	SIZE OF GROUP	MATERIAL REQUIRED
2–5 minutes.	Unlimited.	Prepared slips of paper.

Overview

A short activity designed to form groups of 3 or 4 participants randomly.

Goals

1. To break participants randomly into groups of 3 or 4.
2. To get participants moving around.

Procedure

1. Advise participants that they are going to break into groups.
2. Hand each of them a slip of paper with a number on it along with a piece of information/clue. They should now find other participants with the same number on their slips.

3. Once all of the pieces are together they are to look at the information/clue on their slips and try to determine what the item is that the clues refer to.
4. The first group with a correct answer wins and may be awarded a prize.

Discussion points

1. Who got it right first?
2. What made it easy?
3. What made it hard?

Variations

1. All groups can be awarded a prize when they solve their puzzle.
2. Other pieces of information/clues may be used. Perhaps information from the program.

TRAINER'S NOTES

Only use first three clues for groups of three.

What Am I?

1. I'm soft on top.
1. I'm crunchy on the bottom.
1. I'm cold.
1. I've got a pointy end.

2. Sometimes I crash.
2. I can write letters.
2. I am used most days.
2. I can play games.

3. I'm bitter.
3. I'm light in colour.
3. I'm roundish.
3. I sit in a bowl.

4. I'm square.
4. People stare at me.
4. I'm usually colourful.
4. I get turned on and off.

5. Most people love me.
5. I'm used every day.
5. I have numbers all over me.
5. I sit in pockets.

6. I'm round.
6. I have a handle.
6. People drink with me.
6. Sometimes I get hot.

7. I have three main colours.
7. I control situations.
7. You only see one colour at a time.
7. I frustrate some people.

8. I'm rectangular.
8. I open and close.
8. People strike me.
8. I have sticks inside with coloured tips.

9. I have four legs.
9. People sit on me.
9. I have a vertical back.
9. I am usually covered with cloth.

10. I go up.
10. I move people.
10. I have a tail.
10. I have lots of windows.

48

Top Gun

ITCMXLPES

TIME REQUIRED	SIZE OF GROUP	MATERIAL REQUIRED
60–90 minutes.	Unlimited, but needs to be broken into subgroups of 5–7 participants.	One Top Gun trophy. Each team will require the following: an egg (uncooked in shell), 2 balloons, a pair of scissors, a ruler, 4 ruled index cards, 4 elastic bands, 10 straws, 6 paper clips, 2 polystyrene cups, 10 cm sticky tape, 6 sheets of newspaper, 1 m string. (Place each group's kit in separate disposable shopping bags.)

Overview

An interesting and fun activity that can be linked into almost any situation/topic. It may be used for team building, communication, management development, customer service and so on.

Goals

1. To have the group work together in teams.
2. To participate in a problem-solving activity.
3. To encourage the group.
4. To have lots of fun!

Procedure

1. Start by breaking the large group into smaller teams of 5–7 members.
2. Tell the groups that they will be participating in a competitive activity. They will be given a kit of materials. Using only the material supplied in the kit, they are to construct an 'anti-grenade' that will protect even the shell of an egg from breakage.
3. Tell the groups that after they have constructed their anti-grenade, it must be tested. The test will take place outside (on the roadway, in the hall, on the grass or some other suitable place) and will require them to throw the anti-grenade a distance of four metres (minimum) without breaking the egg inside it. (Every anti-grenade must have an egg inside it.)

4. The teams are now given 30 minutes to construct their anti-grenade. They should also be advised that if they decide to test their design before the real test, any material destroyed will not be replaced.
5. After the construction phase, the teams should be taken to the 'test site' so the evaluation can take place. The winning team should be awarded the Top Gun trophy title. (Be prepared for lots of laughter.)

Discussion points

1. Who won?
2. What went wrong?
3. What assisted the planning phase?
4. What hindered the planning phase?
5. How could you improve the process?
6. How does this apply to the workplace?

Variations

1. Add or delete items in each kit.
2. Have teams estimate how far their anti-grenade can be thrown without the egg inside breaking. These estimates are to be given at the end of the planning period. The team who successfully throws their anti-grenade the estimated distance (or further) wins the award of Top Gun.

TRAINER'S NOTES

1. No catching is allowed.
2. Be aware of noise factor.

89

49

Last Will and Testament

TLPS

TIME REQUIRED	SIZE OF GROUP	MATERIAL REQUIRED
15–30 minutes, depending on numbers.	Unlimited.	A copy of 'My Last Will and Testament' and a pen for each participant.

Overview

A team-building activity designed to allow feedback on personal traits/behaviours.

Goal

1. To allow participants to give feedback to each other on their perceived qualities.

Procedure

1. Inform the group that they are now going to have the opportunity to pass on traits and behaviours to other people in the group.
2. Each person is given a copy of 'My Last Will and Testament' and a pen. They are asked to take 5–10 minutes to identify people in the group to whom they would like to leave certain of their traits/behaviours. They should indicate why they have made their choices.
3. After everyone has finished, allow time for participants to reveal what they have written and why.
4. As a humorous ending, ask people **not** to witness each other's wills or they may become legally binding.

Discussion points

1. Are the perceptions realities?
2. Are the comments fair and constructive?
3. Should we alter our behaviour? Why? Why not?

Variations

1. Pre-named sheets may be handed out. That guarantees one sheet per person.
2. Sheets may be passed around for other people to add to before being revealed.

TRAINER'S NOTES

Ensure constructive comments only.

My Last Will and Testament

I/we being of sound mind revoke all previous wills and testaments and leave the following traits/behaviours to the following people.

Person	Trait	Reason

Signed

Dated

50

Winning Points

TIME REQUIRED	SIZE OF GROUP	MATERIAL REQUIRED
5 minutes.	Unlimited.	None.

Overview

A quick exercise to demonstrate that everyone can win if needs are identified beforehand.

Goal

1. To demonstrate a win/win approach to problem solving.

Procedure

1. Tell everyone that they are going to be involved in a competition.
2. Ask them to stand up and find a partner. The pairs should face each other.
3. Say to the group, 'Think of wishes you would like granted.' Allow 30 seconds to think about this, then say, 'Each time your hand touches your hip, one of your wishes will be granted. Each time your hand touches your partner's hip, one of their

wishes will be granted.' Demonstrate this action if necessary.
4. They now have 30 seconds to obtain as many wishes as they can. 'Ready, set, go!'

Discussion points

1. How many people got all of their wishes met?
2. How many people struggled to get their wishes met?
3. How many people had no wishes met?
4. How does this apply in the workplace?

Variation

1. With a very large group, where you may not have enough space, you may wish to have 2 or 3 pairs volunteer for this exercise and let the others observe.

Source: Conflict Resolution Network, Sydney, Australia.

TRAINER'S NOTES

51

How Much Do You Know #1

ITCMXL

TIME REQUIRED	SIZE OF GROUP	MATERIAL REQUIRED
2 minutes if conducted as an individual exercise; 5–10 minutes if conducted as a group exercise.	Unlimited, but the bigger the better.	Prepared overheads, pen and paper for each participant.

Overview

A quiz designed to be used as an energiser immediately before or after a break.

Goals

1. To fill in time while people come back from breaks.
2. To energise the group.
3. To demonstrate the effect of synergy, if used as a group exercise.

Procedure

1. Tell the group that you are going to give them a quick quiz to test their general knowledge.
2. Let them know that you are going to show them an overhead with 10 questions on it.
3. They will be given 2 minutes to write down as many correct answers as they can.
4. After the 2 minutes are up ask them to stop writing. (Make it as formal as you want.)
5. Show them the correct answers and ask them to check their own answers. Each correct answer is worth 1 point, except that Question 3 is worth 3

points (1 point for each correct area code). The highest possible score is therefore 12.

6. After they have scored their responses ask them who scored 12. Then ask who scored 11 and so on until you get to the highest score. Those who score highest may be awarded a prize.

Discussion point

1. None if it is conducted as an individual exercise, but discussion could be guided towards synergy if it has been a group exercise.

Variations

1. Use different questions.
2. Use trivia questions that relate to the group or their company.
3. After point 4 in the Procedure you could break the group into smaller groups of 5–7 people. Ask them to combine their knowledge and see if the group can do better than the individuals. Show the answers and collect the individual scores together with the group scores for comparison.

TRAINER'S NOTES

General Knowledge Quiz #1

1. Which two countries fought a war from 1980 to 1988?

2. In which country is the volcano Mount Unzen?

3. Which Australian capital cities have the phone area codes 02, 07 and 08?

4. Which green vegetable did George Bush say he disliked and would no longer eat when he became US president?

5. What is the largest planet in our solar system?

6. Which poison is contained in the nuts of apricots?

7. Name the famous riders of the horses Marengo and Copenhagen.

8. A triathlon usually involves which three sports?

9. Angry Anderson was the lead singer of which band?

10. What name is given to the period 1919–1933, when the manufacture and sale of alcohol for common consumption throughout the US was illegal?

General Knowledge Quiz #1—Answers

1. Iran and Iraq

2. Japan

3. 02 = Sydney, Canberra
   07 = Brisbane
   08 = Adelaide, Perth, Darwin

4. Broccoli

5. Jupiter

6. Cyanide

7. Napoleon and Wellington at the battle of Waterloo

8. Swimming, cycling and running

9. Rose Tattoo

10. Prohibition

52

Mixed Bits

ITCMXLP

TIME REQUIRED	SIZE OF GROUP	MATERIAL REQUIRED
20–30 minutes.	Unlimited, but needs to be broken into subgroups of 5–7.	A copy of the 'Mixed Bits' handout and a pen for each group.

Overview

A quick problem-solving activity to demonstrate to the group the benefits of working together.

Goals

1. To get the group working together.
2. To demonstrate the benefits of using group ideas.

Procedure

1. Advise the group that they are going to get involved in a problem-solving activity.
2. The large group now splits into small groups of 5–7 members.
3. Give each group a copy of the 'Mixed Bits' handout.
4. Ask them to work out a way of dividing the symbol shown into 4 parts so that the pieces can be arranged to form a square.

Discussion points

1. Who solved the problem first?
2. What helped the group arrive at the solution?
3. What hindered the group in arriving at the solution?

Variation

1. The problem may be given to individuals first.

Solution

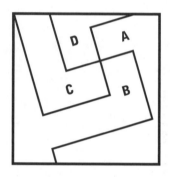

TRAINER'S NOTES

Mixed Bits

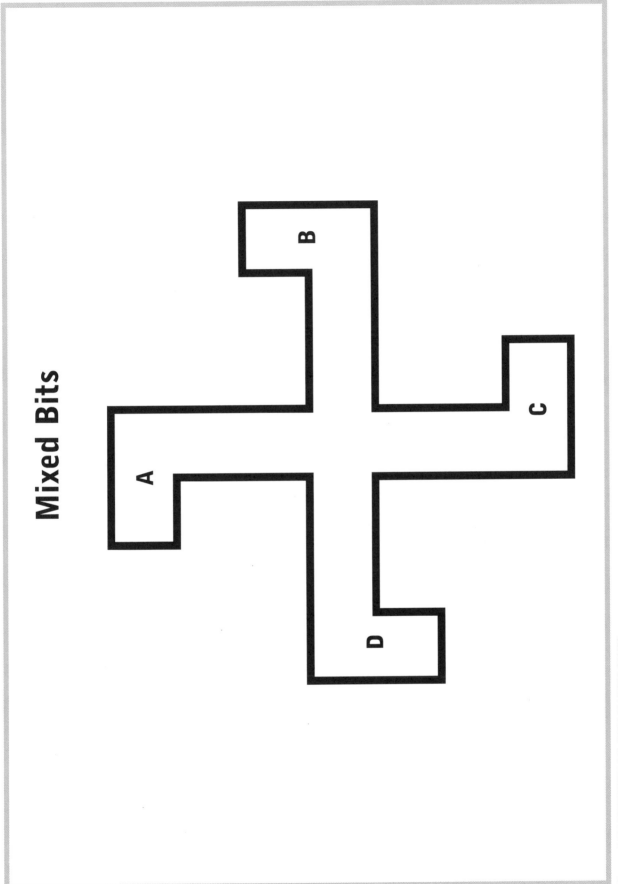

53

Missing Numbers #1

ITCMXL

TIME REQUIRED	SIZE OF GROUP	MATERIAL REQUIRED
10–20 minutes.	Unlimited, but needs to be broken into subgroups of 5–7.	A copy of the 'Missing Numbers' handout and a pen for each group.

Overview

Another quick problem-solving activity to demonstrate the benefits of working together.

Goals

1. To get the group working together.
2. To demonstrate the benefits of using group ideas.

Procedure

1. The group should be broken into small groups of 5–7 people.
2. Give each group a copy of the 'Missing Numbers' handout.
3. Then ask them to use their logic to fill in the missing numbers from the square.

Discussion points

1. Who solved the problem first?
2. What helped the group arrive at the solution?
3. What hindered the group in arriving at a solution?

Variations

You may prefer to have a prepared overhead transparency with the 'Missing Numbers' information displayed.

1	1	1	1	1
1	3	5	7	9
1	5	13	25	41
1	7	25	63	129
1	9	41	129	321

Solution

Each number is the sum of the three numbers immediately above, immediately left and in the upper-left diagonal.

TRAINER'S NOTES

Missing Numbers #1

1				
1	7			
1	5	13		
1	3	5	7	
1	1	1	1	1

54

Balancing Balls

ITCMXL

TIME REQUIRED	SIZE OF GROUP	MATERIAL REQUIRED
5–15 minutes.	Unlimited, but needs to be broken up into subgroups of 5–7 participants.	None, but the facilitator may like to prepare an overhead transparency or flip-chart showing the scales and the eight balls.

Overview

An easy exercise to show the value of using groups to solve problems (synergy).

Goals

1. To allow participants to participate in an activity to demonstrate the benefits of synergy.
2. To encourage communication among group members.

Procedure

1. Advise the group that they are going to be involved in a problem-solving activity.
2. Divide the large group into smaller groups of 5–7 members.
3. Now explain the problem. Each group is to imagine they have a set of scales and eight balls. All balls are the same size and colour, but one is slightly heavier than the others. They are to demonstrate which one of the eight balls is heavier with the use of the scales provided. Sounds easy! The catch is, the scales can only be used twice.
4. Allow 5 minutes for groups to find a solution.

Discussion points

1. Did the groups arrive at a solution?
2. How was the solution identified?
3. How do assumptions affect us? (Refer to game 35.)

Variation

1. Have participants solve the problem individually rather than in groups.

Solution

People usually begin by dividing the balls into 2 groups of 4, which puts them off track immediately. Instead, put 3 balls on each side of the scales. If they are balanced, one of the other balls is heavier. Use the scales to determines which one. If one side is heavier, take those 3 balls. Put 2 of them on the scales. If one is heavier, that's it. If they are both the same it must be the one not on the scales. Easy, isn't it?

TRAINER'S NOTES

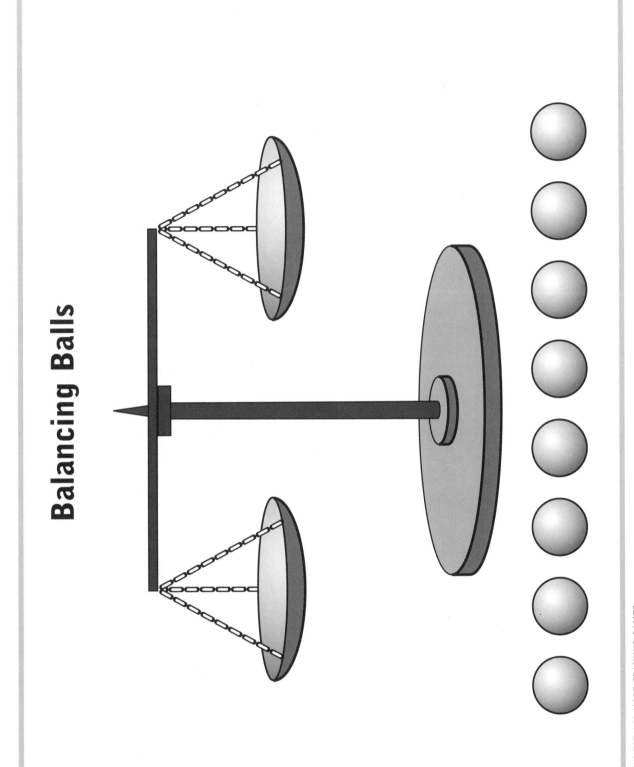

Balancing Balls

55

Mind Reader

ICFMP

TIME REQUIRED	SIZE OF GROUP	MATERIAL REQUIRED
5 minutes.	Unlimited.	None.

Overview

An activity to demonstrate to participants that they may not necessarily be making their own decisions.

Goals

1. To demonstrate to participants that they may not be making decisions by themselves.
2. To demonstrate a form of manipulation to the group.
3. To energise the group.

Procedure

1. Advise the group that they are going to be involved in a quick exercise.
2. Ask everyone to select a number between 2 and 9. This number is to be kept to themselves.
3. Ask them to multiply their selected number by 9. Allow sufficient time for this, depending on the group.
4. Tell participants that if this number has 2 digits, they should add them together.
5. Now ask them to subtract 5 from this amount.
6. They should now relate this number to the letters of the alphabet, so that '1' is the letter 'a', '2' is the letter 'b' and so on.
7. Ask participants to think of a country that starts with that letter.
8. Now ask them to take the second letter of that country and think of an animal starting with that letter. (Before reading any further you may like to try this yourself.)

9. Finally ask, 'How many people were thinking of a grey elephant in Denmark?'

Discussion points

1. How many people had this same solution?
2. How did it happen?
3. Is it manipulation?
4. How does this relate to this training or the workplace?

Variation

1. One person alone from the group could be selected and all others become the audience.

TRAINER'S NOTES

56

My Fantasy

ITCMP

TIME REQUIRED	SIZE OF GROUP	MATERIAL REQUIRED
15–30 minutes.	Unlimited.	A copy of the 'My Fantasy' sheet and a pen for each person.

Overview

An activity which may involve some self-disclosure, but will break down barriers.

Goals

1. To allow participants to share fantasies with each other.
2. To improve communication among participants.
3. To break down some of the barriers that may be in place.
4. To develop more trust between participants.

Procedure

1. Ask each person to think about 3 things they would like to do and 3 things they would like to be. Let the group know that they will not have to share this information if they don't want to, then ask them to write their fantasies on the paper provided.
2. When everyone has completed their lists ask the participants to select the most important one from both lists. They are then to write down at least 3 reasons why these two fantasies are so important.
3. Ask individuals to form small groups (of 2 or 3) to share their fantasies. People who do not want to share their fantasies may be asked to observe/listen to other groups. It might be appropriate to hand them a copy of the discussion points and ask them to start working on them.

Discussion points

1. Can our fantasies come true? Why? Why not?
2. Can or should we support other people in attaining their fantasies?
3. Where do these fantasies fall in existing models? (For example, in Maslow's hierarchy of needs.)

Variations

1. May be conducted in small groups.
2. If you have a very strong, trusting group you may ask them to identify what they believe to be other participants' fantasies.

TRAINER'S NOTES

My Fantasy

I would like to:

1.

2.

3.

Why?

I would like to be:

1.

2.

3.

Why?

57

The Orange

ICMXPES

TIME REQUIRED	SIZE OF GROUP	MATERIAL REQUIRED
5 minutes.	Unlimited.	A flip-chart and an orange (but only if there is one handy).

Overview

A quick story to demonstrate that everyone's needs may be met if the right questions are asked. It deals with conflict resolution.

Goals

1. To look at ways of reducing conflict.
2. To demonstrate how both parties may win if their needs are identified before conflict arises.

Procedure

1. Let the group know that you are going to tell them a story about two little girls. Draw them on the board.
2. Both little girls walked into the kitchen wanting an orange, but found only one orange left on the kitchen table. Illustrate on the board or show them the orange.
3. Ask the group what options the girls have. They should suggest things such as cutting it in half, going and buying an extra one and so on. List these suggestions on the flip-chart.
4. Now ask the group what vital piece of information we need to know but haven't asked for yet. Get ideas from the group until someone suggests that we need to know both of the girls' needs.

5. Had the needs of both girls been known at the start, the solution would have been obvious. This isn't the case in all situations, but it certainly is in some.
6. One girl wanted the rind of the orange to make a cake. The other girl wanted the juice for a drink.
7. Discuss the fact that solutions are sometimes impossible without first establishing the needs of all parties concerned.

Discussion points

1. Why do we tend to go straight for a solution before we identify what the problem is?
2. How does this relate to things at work or at home?
3. How can we overcome this situation?

Variation

1. Use any similar story. For example: A husband and wife both want to use their car right now. Who gets to use it? What are their options? What are their needs? One wants it to go to the shops, the other wants it to pick up the kids. If the needs are identified first, it leads more easily to a solution.

Source: Conflict Resolution Network, Sydney, Australia.

TRAINER'S NOTES

58

Delegation

ICXLPES

TIME REQUIRED	SIZE OF GROUP	MATERIAL REQUIRED
5–10 minutes.	Unlimited.	Prepared overhead transparency or flip-chart with delegation matrix shown.

Overview

An activity designed to show what action may truly be required.

Goals

1. To clarify the distinction between 'urgent' and 'vital'.
2. To indicate which tasks should be done next.
3. To introduce some time-management skills.

Procedure

1. Lead a discussion on the topic of urgency versus importance.
2. A question should be posed as to what should be done first, the vital or urgent things.
3. Display the prepared overhead transparency/flip-chart showing the nine quadrants.

4. Lead a discussion into the importance of each quadrant and what should be done first. The discussion should then flow through to setting priorities.

Discussion points

1. Which quadrant do people normally start working on?
2. Which quadrant should be done first, second, third and so on?
3. Are there any quadrants that shouldn't be done at all?

Variations

1. Handouts may be given to participants with the blank matrix.
2. Participants may be given a list of relevant tasks and then asked to place them on the matrix.

TRAINER'S NOTES

Obviously, both the urgent and important generally do need to be carried out. But people should sometimes question the value of doing urgent tasks. Sometimes a perceived urgency covers the fact that the task may not have any value at all. On the other hand, important tasks will always have value.

Delegation

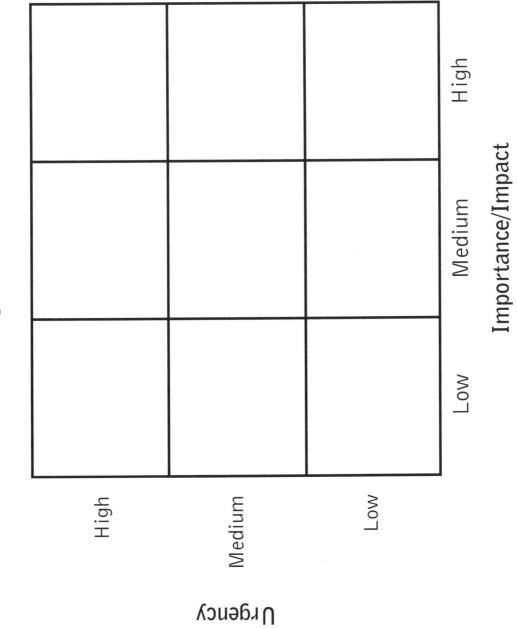

Importance/Impact

High — Medium — Low

Urgency: High — Medium — Low

59

Paperclips

ITCMXLPE

TIME REQUIRED	SIZE OF GROUP	MATERIAL REQUIRED
10–15 minutes.	Unlimited, but need to be broken into smaller groups of 5–7 people.	One paperclip for each group along with enough pens and paper for everyone.

Overview

An activity designed to demonstrate the effects of synergy.

Goals

1. To look at the benefits of synergy.
2. To get the participants to work together.
3. To develop lateral thinking.

Procedure

1. Kick off this activity by handing out pens and paper to each participant.
2. Once all have their writing materials ask them to list as many uses for paperclips as they possibly can. They have 2 minutes to do this and it must be done individually.
3. After participants have completed their lists have the large group form smaller groups of 5–7 people.
4. When the small groups have been formed ask them to compare their individual lists with each other.

5. After the lists have been compared they are then to come up with as many ideas as they can (as a group) in the next 3 minutes.
6. When the 3 minutes are up, get the groups to compare the number of ideas generated as a group with individual scores.

Discussion points

1. Why is it that the groups amassed many more ideas?
2. What caused the extra ideas to come into existence?
3. What helped the group?
4. What hindered the group?
5. How can this apply to the workplace?

Variations

1. Use any other object if paperclips cannot be found.
2. Use an object that the group/company are involved with.

TRAINER'S NOTES

60

Spot the Flaws

ITMXPE

TIME REQUIRED	SIZE OF GROUP	MATERIAL REQUIRED
No extra time required.	Unlimited.	Prepared overheads, pen and paper for each participant.

Overview

A quick activity to get participants thinking. It can be used at any time, but ideally before or after a break.

Goals

1. To energise the group.
2. To have some fun.

Procedure

1. Tell the group that you are going to show them an overhead with two pictures on it.
2. They are to look at the two pictures and try to spot 10 differences between them. They can list them on a piece of paper.
3. The first person to note the 10 differences should let you know.
4. Check to see that they are correct and give them a prize.

Discussion points

1. Who else got high scores?

2. What makes it easier for some people to see the differences than others?

Variations

1. Conduct the same exercise but using something out of a newspaper or magazine. (Check the kids' section first!)
2. Use a photo of the workplace, have it scanned and modified, so you have a 'before' and 'after' shot.

Solution

1. 'Rescue' sign missing from helicopter
2. Blades are different on helicopter
3. Hair is different on man on island
4. Mouth is different on man on island
5. Button missing on cuff of man on island
6. Finger missing from man on island
7. Dog in bottom of boat is not barking
8. Man at back of boat has no tie
9. Second man at front of boat is looking up
10. Missing creature climbing up the island

TRAINER'S NOTES

Spot The Flaws

61

How Much Do You Know? #2

ITCMXL

TIME REQUIRED	SIZE OF GROUP	MATERIAL REQUIRED
2 minutes if used as an individual exercise; 5–10 minutes if used as a group exercise.	Unlimited, but the bigger the better.	Prepared overheads, pen and paper for each participant.

Overview

A quiz for use as an energiser immediately before or after a break.

Goals

1. To fill in time while people come back from breaks.
2. To energise the group.
3. To demonstrate the effect of synergy if used as a group exercise.

Procedure

1. Tell the group that you are going to give them a quick quiz to test their general knowledge.
2. Let them know that you are going to show them an overhead with 10 questions shown on it.
3. They will be given 2 minutes to write down as many correct answers as they can.
4. After the 2 minutes are up ask them to stop writing. (Make it as formal as you want.)
5. Show them the correct answers and ask them to check their own answers. They score 1 point for each correct answer, except that Question 2 is worth 7 points (1 point for each correct wonder) and Question 5 is worth 7 points (1 point for each correct dwarf). The highest possible score would therefore be 22.
6. After they have scored their responses ask them who scored 22. Then ask who scored 21 and so on until you get to the highest score. Those who score highest may be awarded a prize.

Discussion point

1. None if it is conducted as an individual exercise, but discussion could be guided towards synergy if it has been a group exercise.

Variations

1. Use different questions.
2. Use trivia questions that relate to the group or their company.
3. After point 4 in the Procedure you could break the group into smaller groups of 5–7 people. Ask them to combine their knowledge and see if the group can do better than the individuals. Show the answers and collect the individual scores together with the group scores for comparison.

TRAINER'S NOTES

General Knowledge Quiz #2

1. Which organisation was, in 1950, the first to introduce a credit card service?

2. Name the 7 wonders of the world.

3. When and in which city were the first modern Olympic games held?

4. The first sheep were brought into Australia in 1797. Where did they come from?

5. Name the 7 dwarfs.

6. Which metal is the best conductor of electricity?

7. Name the diner where Fonzie, Richie and the gang used to hang out in the television series 'Happy Days'.

8. If travelling at 10 knots, how far from its starting point would a vessel be after an hour?

9. What is the name given to Britain's treasurer?

10. What animal was depicted on the Australian 2¢ coin?

General Knowledge Quiz 2—Answers

1. Diners Club
2. The Egyptian Pyramids
   The Hanging Gardens of Babylon
   The statue of Zeus at Olympia
   The temple of Artemis at Ephesus
   The Mausoleum at Halicarnassus
   The Colossus at Rhodes
   The Pharos (lighthouse) at Alexandria
3. 1896 in Athens
4. The Cape of Good Hope
5. Doc, Sneezy, Grumpy, Happy, Bashful, Sleepy, Dopey
6. Silver
7. Arnold's
8. 10 nautical miles or 11.5 statute (land) miles or 18.5 kilometres
9. The Chancellor of the Exchequer
10. The frill-necked lizard

62

Matches #2

IMXLS

TIME REQUIRED	SIZE OF GROUP	MATERIAL REQUIRED
5 minutes.	Unlimited.	One prepared overhead, or 9 matches with a small group.

Overview

An exercise in lateral thinking and problem solving.

Goals

1. To allow participants to experience an exercise in problem solving.
2. To allow participants to experience an exercise in lateral thinking.
3. To have some fun.

Procedure

1. Tell the group that they are going to be involved in a problem-solving exercise.
2. Show them either the overhead or the 9 matches laid out as shown.
3. Now tell participants that they must move one match but the sum must still read correctly. Allow as much time as needed.
4. Give the winner a prize.

5. Invite discussion of the strategies used to solve this problem. This discussion should be led by participants and should flow into lateral thinking and the use of other people's ideas (i.e. teamwork).

Discussion points

1. How many people found a solution?
2. How many people found more than one solution?
3. Why do most people place limitations on solutions?
4. Why do some people 'give in' so easily?

Variations

1. May be conducted in small groups.
2. Use other items such as drinking straws or strips of paper.

Solution

III − II = I

TRAINER'S NOTES

Matches #2

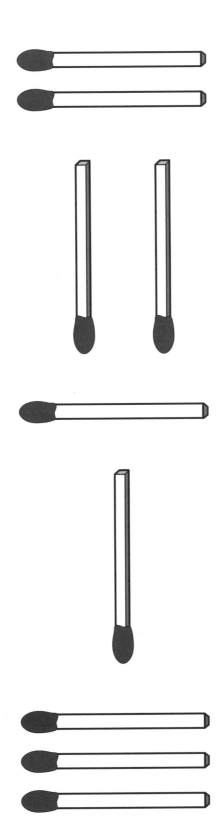

63

Bus Stops

ICFMXPS

TIME REQUIRED	SIZE OF GROUP	MATERIAL REQUIRED
2 minutes.	Unlimited.	Pen and paper for each participant.

Overview

A quick activity designed to show how information overload can interfere with the learning process.

Goal

1. To demonstrate the effect of information overload.

Procedure

1. Tell the group that you are going to tell them a story and at the end you are going to ask them a question about it.
2. Slowly read out the 'Bus Stops' story.
3. After the story has been read out, ask them to write the name of the driver on a piece of paper in front of them.

Discussion points

1. Why didn't everyone know the name of the driver? (Information overload!)
2. What were the essential facts?
3. How does this apply in the workplace?

4. How does this affect our training style?
5. How does this relate to the information we need to give to others?

Variation

1. Use any similar type of story where the same type of opening line can be used.

TRAINER'S NOTES

Bus Stops

You are driving a bus which has 50 people on board. The bus makes a stop, 10 people get off, and 3 get on. At the next stop 8 people get off, and 2 people get on. There are 2 more stops, at which 4 people get off at each. 3 fares get on at one stop and none at the other. At this point the bus has to stop because of mechanical problems. Some of the passengers are in a hurry, so they decide to walk. So 7 people get off the bus. When the mechanical problem is fixed, the bus goes directly to the last stop, and the rest of the people get off.

Question: What was the bus driver's name?

64

What Do We Have Here?

IMP

TIME REQUIRED	SIZE OF GROUP	MATERIAL REQUIRED
No extra time required.	Unlimited.	Prepared overhead.

Overview

A quick perception exercise.

Goals

1. To show that we all have different perceptions.
2. To develop lateral thinking skills.

Procedure

1. Tell the group that you are going to show them an overhead with a picture on it.
2. The first person to tell you what it is will get a prize.

Discussion point

1. Why didn't everyone see it immediately?

Variation

1. Use any picture, scan it, and do a reverse image of it.

Solution

It's a map of the Mediterranean in reverse image. The black is the water and the white is the land. If people still can't see it, point out the 'boot' of Italy.

TRAINER'S NOTES

What Do We Have Here?

65

Hidden Phrases

ICMX

TIME REQUIRED	SIZE OF GROUP	MATERIAL REQUIRED
5 minutes if used as an individual exercise. 10–15 minutes if used as a small group exercise.	Unlimited.	Prepared overheads.

Overview

An activity to show how acronyms or abbreviations can sometimes become confusing.

Goals

1. To demonstrate how abbreviations can become confusing.
2. To energise the group.

Procedure

1. Tell the group you are going to show them a list of 18 abbreviations.
2. They are to write down as many answers as they can in a 2-minute period.
3. The person with the highest number of correct answers should get a prize.

Discussion points

1. How does this relate to us in the workplace?
2. Are we guilty of using abbreviations ourselves without explaining what they are?

Variation

1. After point 2 in the Procedure you could get participants to form groups of 5–7 people and ask them to combine their knowledge and see if the group can do any better than the individuals. Then compare the individual scores with the group scores.

Answers

1. 2 peas in a pod
2. 7 days in a week
3. 7 wonders of the world
4. 1 wheel on a unicycle
5. On top of the world
6. 29 days in February in a leap year
7. 8 sides on a stop sign
8. 4 digits in a postcode
9. 4 suits in a deck of cards
10. 3 blind mice, see how they run
11. 18 holes on a golf course
12. 88 keys on a piano
13. 50 states in the USA
14. 12 signs of the zodiac
15. Somewhere over the rainbow
16. 24 hours in a day
17. The squeaky wheel gets the oil
18. 100 cents in a dollar

TRAINER'S NOTES

What are the hidden phrases?

For example: 52 w. in a y. = 52 weeks in a year

1. 2 p. in a p.

2. 7 d. in a w.

3. 7 w. of the w.

4. 1 w. on a. u.

5. On t. of the w.

6. 29 d. in F. in a l. y.

7. 8 s. on a s. s.

8. 4 d. in a p. c.

9. 4 s. in a d. of c.

10. 3 b. m., s. h. t. r.

11. 18 h. on a g. c.

12. 88 k. on a p.

13. 50 s. in the U.S.

14. 12 s. of the z.

15. s. over the r.

16. 24 h. in a d.

17. The s. w. g. t. o.

18. 100 c. in a d.

66

The Interview

CMPS

TIME REQUIRED	SIZE OF GROUP	MATERIAL REQUIRED
15–30 minutes.	Up to 18–20.	None.

Overview

An activity to highlight the importance of giving people an overview of things.

Goals

1. To allow participants to see how confusing something can be without getting an overview.
2. To show participants ways of improving communication.

Procedure

1. Ask for four volunteers.
2. Ask one of these people to leave the room. The other three should prepare to interview the person who has just left the room. They are to interview the person for an unusual position, the nature of which they are to decide (e.g. weapons inspector, wine taster, test pilot). However, they should NOT divulge the nature of the position during the interview. Allow 5 minutes for preparation.
3. Call the person in from outside and advise them that they are going to be interviewed for a position. They are to answer all questions as they

are asked and must try to guess what the position is during the interview.

Discussion points

1. How did the interviewee feel during the interview?
2. How easy was it to guess what the position was? Why? Why not?
3. Does it improve general communication if everyone knows the whole picture?
4. How does this activity relate to everyday situations?

Variations

1. A number of interviews may be conducted at the same time.
2. A prepared list of occupations may be given to the interviewing committee.
3. The interviewee may just listen to the questions without answering them.
4. The audience may also be required to guess the position being interviewed for.

TRAINER'S NOTES

67

Team Names

TIME REQUIRED	SIZE OF GROUP	MATERIAL REQUIRED
20–30 minutes.	Unlimited, but needs to be broken into subgroups of 5–7 participants.	None, but participants may like to find suitable items if they wish.

Overview

An activity to allow groups to form an initial bond.

Goals

1. To identify each small group.
2. To encourage communication.
3. To allow individuals in each group to bond.
4. To have fun!

Procedure

1. Divide the group into smaller groups of 5–7 members.
2. Ask each group to come up with a name for itself. The name may be practical or symbolic—leave the choice entirely up to the group and give them 10 minutes.

3. When the groups have finished, ask them to introduce themselves, the group name and the reason/s for their selection. These group names should be used for the duration of the course where applicable.

Discussion points

1. What were the names?
2. Did they accurately describe the group?
3. Will this exercise improve the course? Why? Why not?

Variation

1. Group members could be rotated during the program.

TRAINER'S NOTES

68

Preconceived

CFLP

TIME REQUIRED	SIZE OF GROUP	MATERIAL REQUIRED
30–60 minutes.	Unlimited, but needs to be broken into subgroups of 5–7 people.	A set of category cards prepared from page 125, a sheet of flip-chart paper and a marker for each group.

Overview

This activity has been designed to allow participants to explore stereotypes and prejudices.

Goals

1. To present an opportunity to discuss some of the preconceived ideas people have.
2. To look at some of the stereotypes people have and also to dispel these misconceptions.

Procedure

1. Divide the group into subgroups of 5–7 people.
2. Give each group one category card, a sheet of flip-chart paper and a marker.
3. Now ask each group to think of all of the stereotypes, preconceptions, stock reactions they know of concerning these categories. They should list them all on the flip-chart paper. Allow 5 minutes for this.
4. After the groups have finished their lists, post the sheets on a wall.
5. Each category should now be discussed and all of the stereotypes and preconceptions dismissed, preferably by the participants themselves.

Discussion points

1. Why do some people have these preconceived ideas?
2. Why do some people have prejudices?
3. How can we improve the situation?

Variations

1. May be conducted on an individual basis rather than in small groups.
2. The exercise can be conducted verbally rather than in written form.
3. Groups or individuals may be given more than one category.
4. Use different categories.

Categories

Aboriginals	Doctors	Police
Arabs	Foreigners	Plumbers
Blacks	Gays	Punks
Bus conductors	Gypsies	Smokers
Car salespeople	Irish	Tourists
Catholics	Jews	Trainers
Country folk	Men	Truck drivers
Cyclists	Old people	Women

TRAINER'S NOTES

Categories (victims of preconceptions)

Aboriginals	Doctors	Police
Arabs	Foreigners	Plumbers
Blacks	Gays	Punks
Bus conductors	Gypsies	Smokers
Car salespeople	Irish	Tourists
Catholics	Jews	Trainers
Country folk	Men	Truck drivers
Cyclists	Old people	Women

69

Airport

LES

TIME REQUIRED	SIZE OF GROUP	MATERIAL REQUIRED
10–20 minutes.	Unlimited, but needs to be broken into subgroups of 5–7 participants.	A whiteboard and marker or flip-chart and marker for the facilitator. A sheet of paper and pen for each group.

Overview

An unusual activity to be used at the beginning of a program, designed to allow participants to introduce themselves and to start thinking about their expectations and desired outcomes.

Goals

1. To give participants the opportunity to introduce themselves and find out about some of the other people.
2. To encourage participants to focus on their expectations of the program and also focus on what they would like to be able to take away with them.

Procedure

1. Divide the group into smaller groups of 5–7 people.
2. After the groups have been formed, tell them that they are all sitting at an airport waiting to catch a plane. Unfortunately, due to the current weather conditions, aircraft are not taking off or landing. As their group members are all waiting to catch the same flight, they may as well take some time to get to know each other.
3. Make an analogy between the trip the participants are meant to be taking and the course. As they introduce themselves, they should identify the things that they would like to see on their trip (the course). They should also identify the things they would like to take home with them (the outcomes).
4. Give groups 5–10 minutes to act out the role-play.

Discussion points

1. Are all of these expectations relevant? Can we add to/delete some of them?
2. Which are the most important?
3. Which are the least important?

Variation

1. List all expectations and post them somewhere in the room for the duration of the program. At the conclusion, this list may be used as an evaluation tool: did the program satisfy the needs originally identified?

TRAINER'S NOTES

70

Balancing Glasses

TMXP

TIME REQUIRED	SIZE OF GROUP	MATERIAL REQUIRED
10–15 minutes.	Unlimited, but needs to be broken into subgroups of 5–7 participants.	Three glasses and an A4 sheet of paper for each group.

Overview

A simple problem-solving activity to get people moving and thinking.

Goals

1. To demonstrate to participants the effect of synergy.
2. To encourage communication among participants.
3. To energise the group.
4. To look at a problem-solving process.

Procedure

1. Begin this activity by breaking the larger group into subgroups of 5–7 people.
2. Give each group 3 glasses and an A4 sheet of paper.
3. Ask the participants to balance one of the glasses on top of the piece of paper, which in turn is to be balanced on the other two glasses. The upper glass should not be resting on the rims of either of the other 2 glasses, but on the paper alone. Allow 5–10 minutes for this stage.
4. After the time has elapsed, ask any group which has not found a solution to stop.
5. Solutions and feedback should be elicited from the groups. This will lead into the topic area or simply reinforce the fact that participants should work together to get the best results.

Discussion points

1. Who found a solution?
2. How many solutions were there?
3. What assisted the group in arriving at a solution?
4. What hindered the group in arriving at a solution?
5. How does this activity relate to this program/workplace?

Variations

1. To make the task a little more difficult, this could be conducted as a non-verbal exercise.
2. To make the task a little more difficult, the top glass can be filled with water.
3. After point 3 in the Procedure, if none of the groups has found a solution tell them to fold the sheet of paper if they need to, then give them a few more minutes.

Solution

Fanfold the paper.

TRAINER'S NOTES

Balancing Glasses

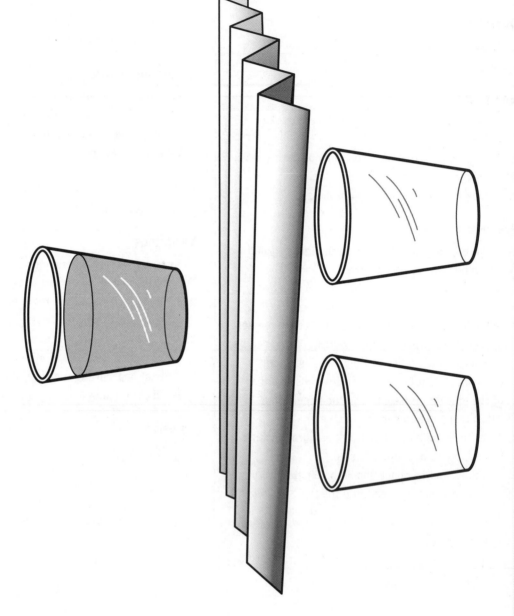

71

How Much Do You Know #3

ITCMXL

TIME REQUIRED	SIZE OF GROUP	MATERIAL REQUIRED
2 minutes if used as an individual exercise; 5–10 minutes if used as a group exercise.	Unlimited, but the bigger the better.	Prepared overheads, pen and paper for each participant.

Overview

A quiz for use as an energiser immediately before or after a break.

Goals

1. To fill in time while people come back from breaks.
2. To energise the group.
3. To demonstrate the effect of synergy if used as a group exercise.

Procedure

1. Tell the group that you are going to give them a quick quiz to test their general knowledge.
2. Let them know that you are going to show them an overhead with 10 questions shown on it.
3. They will be given 2 minutes to write down as many correct answers as they can.
4. After the 2 minutes are up ask them to stop writing. (Make it as formal as you want.)
5. Show them the correct answers and ask them to check their own answers. They score 1 point for each correct answer, except that Question 5 is worth 4 points (1 point for each correct city). The highest possible score would therefore be 13.
6. After they have scored their responses ask them who scored 13. Then ask who scored 12 and so on until you get to the highest score. Those who score highest may be awarded a prize.

Discussion points

1. None if it is conducted as an individual exercise, but discussion could be guided towards synergy if it has been a group exercise.

Variations

1. Use different questions.
2. Use trivia questions that relate to the group or their company.
3. After point 4 in the Procedure you could break the group into smaller groups of 5–7 people. Ask them to combine their knowledge and see if the group can do better than the individuals. Show the answers and collect the individual scores together with the group scores for comparison.

TRAINER'S NOTES

General Knowledge Quiz #3

1. In American slang, what does a 'Fin' constitute in U.S. currency?

2. Who sang the title song on the soundtrack of the 1966 Michael Caine film, Alfie?

3. Which Caribbean island nation is divided into three counties—Surrey, Middlesex and Cornwall?

4. Which of Agatha Christie's novels is set on a river steamer?

5. Name the four cities, all beginning with the same letter, that hosted consecutive Olympic games.

6. What is the first name of Agatha Christie's detective, Miss Marple?

7. What creature is depicted on the flag of Wales?

8. Oenology is the study of what liquids?

9. What name is given to the container from which cards are drawn and dealt in the games of blackjack and baccarat?

10. How many left-handed riders are permitted in a polo team?

General Knowledge Quiz #3—Answers

1. $5

2. Cilla Black

3. Jamaica

4. Death on the Nile

5. Mexico City in 1968
   Munich in 1972
   Montreal in 1976
   Moscow in 1980

6. Jane

7. A dragon

8. Wines

9. Shoe

10. None

72

Missing Numbers #2

ITCMXL

TIME REQUIRED	SIZE OF GROUP	MATERIAL REQUIRED
10–15 minutes.	Unlimited, but needs to be broken into subgroups of 5–7.	A prepared overhead or a copy of the 'Missing Numbers' handout and a pen for each group.

Overview

Another quick problem-solving activity to demonstrate the benefits of working together.

Goals

1. To get the group working together.
2. To demonstrate the benefits of using group ideas.

Procedure

1. Divide the group into smaller groups of 5–7 people.
2. Give each group a copy of the 'Missing Numbers' handout.
3. Then ask them to use logic to fill in the missing numbers from the square.
4. Give the winning group a prize.

Discussion points

1. Who solved the problem first?
2. What helped the group arrive at the solution?
3. What hindered the group in arriving at a solution?

Variations

You may prefer to have a prepared overhead transparency with the 'Missing Numbers' information displayed.

Solution

8	1	6
3	5	7
4	9	2

All verticals, horizontals and diagonals total 15.

TRAINER'S NOTES

Missing Numbers #2

8	1	?
3	5	?
4	9	?

73
Alphabet Soup #2

ITCMX

TIME REQUIRED	SIZE OF GROUP	MATERIAL REQUIRED
No extra time required as an individual exercise; 5–10 minutes if used as a small group exercise.	Unlimited.	Prepared overhead.

Overview

A fun activity that can be used at any time during training for a change of pace.

Goals

1. To energise the group.
2. If used in a small group situation, to involve them in a very quick problem-solving activity.

Procedure

1. Tell the group that they are going to be involved in a quick problem-solving exercise.
2. They are going to be shown a sentence on an overhead. Their job is to fill in the 26 blanks using each letter of the alphabet only once.
3. Show the overhead until someone gets the correct answer.
4. Award a prize.

Discussion points

(None, unless conducted as a small group exercise.)
1. What helped the group arrive at the solution?
2. What hindered the group in arriving at a solution?
3. How can this apply to us in the workplace?

Variation

1. After point 2 in the Procedure give individuals 30 seconds each, then form them into small groups of 5–7 people and ask the group to solve the problem.

Solution

The crazy musician was always very quick to jump aboard the ferry on exactly the right quay.

TRAINER'S NOTES

_he _ra_y _u_icia_ was _l_ays

_er_ qu_c_ t_ um_ th_ e_ry on

_a_oar_ e_ry ri_ht _e_

e_act_y t_ _ay.

74

PART Game

TCFMLPES

TIME REQUIRED	SIZE OF GROUP	MATERIAL REQUIRED
10–15 minutes.	Unlimited, but a minimum of around 10–12.	Four prepared cards marked 'P', 'A', 'R' and 'T' and a copy of the 'PART Game Score Sheet' for each participant.

Overview

This activity has been designed to show how people have different learning styles.

Goals

1. To demonstrate practically four different learning styles.
2. To get participants to identify their own preferred learning style.
3. To get participants up and moving about.

Procedure

1. Start off by leading a discussion into the different styles of learning that people may have.
2. Advise the group that you are now going to show them their own preferred learning styles.
3. Ask the group to stand up and hand each of them a copy of the 'PART Game Score Sheet'.
4. Place the 4 prepared cards in each corner of the room or other areas distant from each other.
5. Tell the group that you are now going to read out 12 statements. Each statement will have 4 possible responses.
6. When they make a choice of response they should place a tick in the appropriate column on their score sheet. For example, if they choose the third response to the first statement then they should place a tick in the 'R' column of their score sheet.

7. Now read out the 12 statements in turn, making sure that everyone is following and has time to select a response and mark their sheets.
8. After you have read out the 12 statements get them to total up the ticks in each of the 4 columns.
9. Tell them that the highest total of the 4 columns indicates their preferred learning style. Also point out that our preferred learning style is also the one we tend to use as trainers and that it may interfere with some of the trainees' styles.
10. Read out or give a talk based on the 'Learning Styles—General Descriptions' sheet.
11. A discussion can now be initiated into how these different learning styles affect us as trainers.

Discussion points

1. How does this affect us as trainers?
2. What happens if we use the same style all of the time?
3. What type of learning style should we work with?
4. Is it possible to use all 4 styles?

Variation

1. Use different statements/questions if necessary, but make sure they all have the same types of responses.

Source: Jude Pettitt, Kim Davis and Barbara Albany, Sydney, Australia.

TRAINER'S NOTES

Sometimes people can't decide on a single response to the statements. If this is the case allow them to make 2 ticks.

PART Game Questions (1)

1. When assembling a pushbike or a garden fitting you would prefer to:

P have someone with experience show you the most important stages of assembly and give you simple, effective instructions.

A turn the box upside-down in the lounge room and assemble it immediately so you can use it as soon as possible.

R take as much time as necessary to read the instruction manual, get the necessary tools and talk with friends about the task.

T carefully read all of the instructions and arrange all parts in sequential order, ensuring that all parts are there and undamaged before attempting the assembly.

2. When you have a month to complete a project you would prefer to:

P follow an existing format or timetable which allows the project to be completed one step at a time.

A work in bursts when you feel inspired and enthusiastic about the task.

R work on it with others and preferably when you feel like it.

T carefully plan how you will complete the task and then develop a systematic, ordered approach, probably doing a little each day.

3. When someone gives you a new recipe you would prefer to:

P try the recipe out and look for ways that it might be made simpler or better along the way. You might also prefer to test it first or have had it recommended to you.

A begin to cook only checking the recipe briefly for main instructions, often improvising and experimenting.

R compare the recipe to others you have tried and then consider the merits of each before you decide to go ahead.

T read the recipe several times, measuring and preparing all the ingredients in advance and following the directions provided in the recipe.

4. When preparing for a holiday you tend to:

P find out from friends the best way to travel and then make quick decisions on what are the most practical and useful things to take with you.

A pack quickly and at the last minute, knowing whatever you have forgotten can be bought when you get there.

R explore all of your travel options, leaving plenty of time to make decisions and arrangements after giving it careful consideration.

T study all the travel guides, maps, itineraries and use a checklist to assist you with the packing and planning.

5. Do you tend to relate best to information that is:

P practical and useful.
A interesting and inventive.
R personally relevant.
T factual and logical.

6. When arriving home with a new video player you would prefer to:

P unpack the video, plug it in, read part of the manual and then experiment with how it works, checking back to the manual for each new step.

A unpack the video, quickly plug it in and call your neighbour to help.

R carefully read the instructions and arrange for a technician or friend to install it so you can watch how it's done.

T read the entire manual and any other relevant material before attempting the installation.

PART Game Questions (2)

7. If you were asked to prepare a report of your organisation you would prefer to:

P identify and list the problem areas and note how they could be ameliorated to increase productivity.

A develop a flow chart showing how the organisation interrelates with the community and state bodies.

R create a map connecting the people involved and how they relate to each other.

T prepare an organisational chart showing the organisational structure and chain of command.

8. When faced with a decision you prefer to:

P consider all your options one by one, then use a method that you have developed in the past and know works.

A make a snap decision and see what happens; you can always change it if it's not right.

R discuss it with people close to you, considering their needs, then make a decision that feels best for you.

T analyse all of your options and prioritise them before thinking about the best decision.

9. You are most comfortable with people who:

P provide practical advice and offer alternatives.

A are people of action, who get out into the world and do things.

R share your values about the world and take time to reflect on things.

T are intellectually competent.

10. You feel that students would learn much more effectively if:

P teachers provided them with information that was practical and useful in their lives.

A teachers encouraged creativity and initiative in the classroom.

R teachers spent more time acknowledging feelings and ensuring that information was relevant.

T teachers made better use of the time available by being better organised and providing accurate, detailed and factual information.

11. When working with people who are distressed you find it most frustrating when:

P they don't allow themselves to stay with the problem, they keep putting it aside.

A they don't act on what they must know instinctively is the best course of action.

R they don't allow themselves to be emotionally expressive.

T they don't just stop and logically think through their options.

12. When you have a large report to write, you would prefer to:

P follow an existing format or timetable you have used in the past that will allow the report to be completed one step at a time.

A work on it in short bursts when you feel inspired and enthusiastic.

R work on it with other people when you feel like it.

T plan how you will complete the report step by step, then work out what to do each day.

PART Game Score Sheet

Instructions: Place a tick in the relevant columns under P, A, R or T each time you select a response from the statements given. After all 12 statements have been competed, total each column.

	P	A	R	T
1				
2				
3				
4				
5				
6				
7				
8				
9				
10				
11				
12				
Totals				

Notes:

Learning Styles—General Descriptions

Pragmatists

- are keen to try out ideas, theories and techniques to see if they work in practice
- search out new ideas and take the first opportunity to use them
- like to get on with things
- tend to be impatient
- are practical, down-to-earth people who like making practical decisions and solving problems
- respond to problems and opportunities as a challenge
- believe that 'There is always a better way' and 'If it works it's good'.

Activists

- involve themselves fully and without bias in new experiences
- are open-minded
- are enthusiastic about anything new
- tend to act first and consider consequences afterwards
- fill their days with activities
- like to be in the middle of things
- believe that you should try anything once.

Reflectors

- like to stand back and ponder experiences
- like to collect data and analyse it before coming to conclusions
- tend to postpone reaching a definitive conclusion because of data collection
- like to consider all possible angles and implications before making a move
- prefer to watch others in action, taking a back seat
- act with a view to the wider context
- believe in being cautious.

Theorists

- adapt and integrate observations into complex but logically sound theories
- think problems through in a step-by-step, logical way
- tend to be perfectionists
- are keen on basic assumptions, principles, theories, models and systems thinking
- tend to be detached, analytical and dedicated to rational objectivity
- prefer to maximise certainty and are uncomfortable with subjective judgement and lateral thinking
- believe in rationality and logic: 'If it's logical it's good'.

PART

75

Six

ICMXLPS

TIME REQUIRED	SIZE OF GROUP	MATERIAL REQUIRED
No extra time required.	Unlimited.	Prepared overhead or flip-chart sheet.

Overview

A very quick lateral thinking activity which may also be used to fill in time before or after a break.

Goals

1. To demonstrate how a perception or mind set can interfere with the solving of a simple problem.
2. To get participants involved in lateral thinking.

Procedure

1. Tell the group that you are going to show them the roman numeral for the number 9.
2. Ask them to change it to the number 6 using a single line.
3. The first person to solve the problem gets a prize.

Discussion points

1. Who got the first solution?
2. Is there more than one solution to the problem?
3. What stopped everyone from coming up with an answer?

Variation

1. Ask the participants to write their answers on a piece of paper as they solve the problem. Wait for about a minute then ask the people who didn't get a solution, what they were doing to solve it.

Solution

Put an 'S' in front of the 'IX'. Your instructions didn't say that it had to be a straight line.

TRAINER'S NOTES

76

16 Squares

IMP

TIME REQUIRED	SIZE OF GROUP	MATERIAL REQUIRED
2–5 minutes.	Unlimited.	Prepared overhead or flip-chart sheet.

Overview

A very quick activity to demonstrate how lateral thinking can improve results, and to show how trying to come up with a fast answer can sometimes lead to errors in our calculations.

Goals

1. To get participants to think laterally.
2. To show that speed can affect quality.
3. To fill in time before or after a break.

Procedure

1. Tell the group that they are going to take part in a quick problem-solving activity.
2. Show them the overhead of the 16 squares and then ask how many squares are located inside the heavy-lined square.
3. The first correct answer is awarded a prize.

Discussion point

1. Why do some people see all of the squares and other people only some of them?

Variation

1. See Games 77 and 78.

Solution

The obvious answer is 16, but there are 16 squares that are 1 x 1

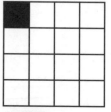

there are 9 squares that are 2 x 2

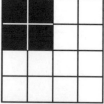

there are 4 squares that are 3 x 3

and there is 1 square that is 4 x 4.

Therefore the correct answer is 30.

TRAINER'S NOTES

How Many Squares?

77

25 Squares

TIME REQUIRED	SIZE OF GROUP	MATERIAL REQUIRED
2–5 minutes.	Unlimited.	Prepared overhead or flip-chart sheet.

Overview

A very quick activity to demonstrate how lateral thinking can improve results, and to show how trying to come up with a fast answer can sometimes lead to errors in our calculations. This can be used some time after Game 76 to prove a point.

Goals

1. To reinforce the outcome of Game 76.
2. To get participants to think laterally.
3. To show that speed can affect quality.
4. To fill in time before or after a break.

Procedure

1. Tell the group that they are going to take part in another quick problem-solving activity.
2. Show them the overhead of the 25 squares and then ask how many squares are located inside the heavy-lined square.
3. The first correct answer is awarded a prize.

Discussion point

1. Were better results achieved this time?

Variation

1. See Games 76 and 78.

Solution

The obvious answer is 25, but there are 25 squares that are 1 x 1

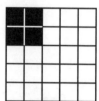

there are 16 squares that are 2 x 2

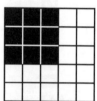

there are 9 squares that are 3 x 3

there are 4 squares that are 4 x 4

and there is 1 square that is 5 x 5.

Therefore the correct answer is 55.

TRAINER'S NOTES

How Many Squares?

78

Triangles

IMP

TIME REQUIRED	SIZE OF GROUP	MATERIAL REQUIRED
2–5 minutes.	Unlimited.	Prepared overhead or flip-chart sheet.

Overview

Another quick activity to demonstrate how lateral thinking can improve results, and to show how trying to come up with a fast answer can sometimes lead to errors in our calculations. This can be used some time after Games 76 and 77 to prove a point.

Goals

1. To reinforce the outcome of Games 76 and 77.
2. To get participants to think laterally.
3. To show that speed can affect quality.
4. To fill in time before or after a break.

Procedure

1. Tell the group that they are going to take part in another quick problem-solving activity.
2. Show them the overhead of the pentagon and then ask how many triangles are located inside the pentagon.
3. The first correct answer is awarded a prize.

Discussion points

1. Were better results achieved this time?
2. Does a systematic approach help to solve problems more easily?

Variation

1. See Games 76 and 77.

Solution

There are:
5 small triangles (AFG)
5 small triangles (AGB)
5 tall triangles (ABD)
5 long base triangles (ACJ)
5 triangles with 2 external sides (EAB)
10 triangles with 2 small sides inside (ABF)

Therefore the correct answer is 35.

TRAINER'S NOTES

How Many Triangles?

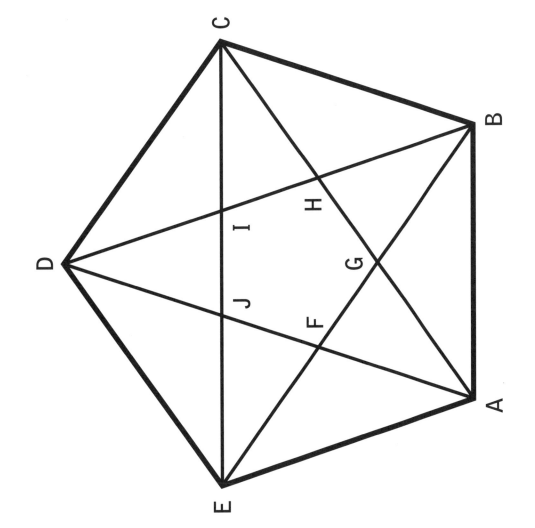

79

Scavenger Hunt

IT

TIME REQUIRED	SIZE OF GROUP	MATERIAL REQUIRED
Depends on the size of groups and availability of requested items.	Unlimited, but needs to be broken into smaller teams of 5–7 people.	A handout of the 'Scavenger Hunt' list for each team.

Overview

This activity is designed to be used before a long training course commences, or to break up a long program.

Goals

1. To develop a team approach.
2. To see how resourceful team members are.
3. To energise the group.

Procedure

1. Divide the group into teams of 5–7 people.
2. Tell the participants that they are all going to go on a scavenger hunt. A prize will be awarded to the winning team.
3. Give the 'Scavenger Hunt' list to the teams. Tell them that they are to use their own resources to get as many of the items shown as possible.
4. Set a time limit, say 1 hour.

5. When the time is up, get everybody back together and see which team has the highest number of items.

Discussion points

1. How close were the other teams to finishing?
2. How do you feel about the winning team?
3. Did anyone in your team appear to be more resourceful or cunning than anyone else?
4. Did anyone in your team take charge? Who? Why?

Variations

1. Give the list out 24 hours before the training starts. Advise each team that one of the first things to be done when the training commences is to find out the results of the Scavenger Hunt. This technique will develop a teamwork approach even before training commences.
2. Come up with other items for the Scavenger Hunt. A blank form can be found on page 153.

TRAINER'S NOTES

Scavenger Hunt (1)

		Item	Points
❑	1.	A coloured condom	4
❑	2.	An ice cube	4
❑	3.	A postcard from interstate	8
❑	4.	10 paperclips	6
❑	5.	6 oak leaves	7
❑	6.	A bald tyre	8
❑	7.	A bank statement	1
❑	8.	A black jelly baby	4
❑	9.	A contraceptive pill	4
❑	10.	A cow pat (fresh)	7
❑	11.	A company envelope	2
❑	12.	A Phillips™ screwdriver	6
❑	13.	A raw potato	2
❑	14.	A stranger (female)	10
❑	15.	A stranger (male)	10
❑	16.	A telephone (not a mobile phone)	5
❑	17.	A Yale key	1
❑	18.	A video of Queen Elizabeth	8
❑	19.	A Beatles cassette	6
❑	20.	A bus ticket	7
❑	21.	A cake fork	3
❑	22.	A Christmas card (blank)	6
❑	23.	A coloured light globe	5
❑	24.	A $5\frac{1}{4}''$ floppy disk	4

Scavenger Hunt (2)

	Item	Points
❏	25. An empty chocolate milk container	2
❏	26. A piece of foreign currency	9
❏	27. A highlighter pen	2
❏	28. A jar of blackberry jam	2
❏	29. A pair of handcuffs	10
❏	30. A photo of John Cleese	6
❏	31. A piece of coal	3
❏	32. A plastic cup	1
❏	33. A police officer's hat	10
❏	34. A large roll of Sellotape	3
❏	35. A set of dentures	5
❏	36. A piece of sheet music	6
❏	37. A spider in a jar (live)	9
❏	38. Last Tuesday's paper	6
❏	39. Tomorrow's paper	10
❏	40. A traffic infringement notice	8
❏	41. A train ticket	7
❏	42. A used postage stamp	2
❏	43. A whip	10
❏	44. 6 men's ties	5
❏	45. A team theme song which everyone must sing together to get the points	6

Highest possible score for all 45 items = 250

Scavenger Hunt

Item	Points

80

Likes and Gripes

TIME REQUIRED	SIZE OF GROUP	MATERIAL REQUIRED
30–45 minutes, but will depend on the size of the group and how far the facilitator wants to stay with it.	Unlimited.	A copy of the 'Likes and Gripes' handout and a pen for everyone.

Overview

This is an activity that allows participants to pass comment on others without any threat. It is most suitable for groups who are part of the same team or department at work, or groups who know each other well.

Goals

1. To allow participants to comment on others without any threat.
2. To give feedback to all participants on their perceived behaviours or traits.

Procedure

1. Let participants know that they are going to have an opportunity to give everyone else in the group feedback on their behaviours and traits, that is, the things you like and dislike about the person. The facilitator should also be part of the process.
2. Advise everyone that this is an anonymous activity and that no one will be asked who wrote specific comments about anyone else.
3. Give everyone a copy of the 'Likes and Gripes' handout and ask them to put at least one like and dislike for each person in the group.

4. Collects all sheets, mix them and then read through the comments for each person, one at a time. You should start with your own name first.
5. Request feedback from the group as to the accurateness of the comments made.
6. Lead the discussion into teamwork and the different roles that have to be assumed in order for a team to function properly.

Discussion points

1. Are all of the comments accurate?
2. Were there any conflicting comments made? Why? How could this be?
3. Does anyone now want to punch anyone out?

Variations

1. All of the group members' names can be shown on the handout before being copied for the participants.
2. The facilitator can retain the completed sheets away at point 4 in the Procedure and summarise the comments before discussion. This allows the facilitator to screen the comments and reduce the chances of serious conflict.
3. If a summary is made by the facilitator, the debriefing can be done by one of the group members.

TRAINER'S NOTES

Be aware of conflict with this exercise. If there is a chance that some people will use this activity as a slander session you may want to set more rigid guidelines.

Likes and Gripes

There are things you like about the individuals you work with, such as their tidiness, their sense of humour and their friendship. There are also things you don't like about them, such as their lack of concern for others, lack of loyalty or rudeness.

Take a few minutes to think about everyone in the group, including the course facilitator(s) (if appropriate), and write down at least one thing you like about them and one thing you dislike about them.

Your name is not required. The lists may be summarised and passed around later in the course, but you will **not** be asked to identify the comments you have made! Please make sure your handwriting is legible.

Who?	What I like about them	What I dislike about them

81

How Much Do You Know? #4

ITCMXL

TIME REQUIRED	SIZE OF GROUP	MATERIAL REQUIRED
2 minutes if used as an individual exercise; 5–10 minutes if used as a group exercise.	Unlimited, but the bigger the better.	Prepared overheads, pen and paper for each participant.

Overview

A quiz for use as an energiser immediately before or after a break.

Goals

1. To fill in time while people come back from breaks.
2. To energise the group.
3. To demonstrate the effect of synergy if used as a group exercise.

Procedure

1. Tell the group that you are going to give them a quick quiz to test their general knowledge.
2. Let them know that you are going to show them an overhead with 10 questions shown on it.
3. They will be given 2 minutes to write down as many correct answers as they can.
4. After the 2 minutes are up ask them to stop writing. (Make it as formal as you want.)
5. Show them the correct answers and ask them to check their own answers. They score 1 point for each correct answer, except that Question 5 is worth 4 points (1 point for each correct city). The highest possible score would therefore be 13.
6. After they have scored their responses ask them who scored 13. Then ask who scored 12 and so on until you get to the highest score. Those who score highest may be awarded a prize.

Discussion point

1. None if it is conducted as an individual exercise, but discussion could be guided towards synergy if it has been a group exercise.

Variations

1. Use different questions.
2. Use trivia questions that relate to the group or their company.
3. After point 4 in the Procedure you could break the group into smaller groups of 5–7 people. Ask them to combine their knowledge and see if the group can do better than the individuals. Show the answers and collect the individual scores together with the group scores for comparison.

TRAINER'S NOTES

General Knowledge Quiz #4

1. What name is common to a roofing material and a skin disease?

2. 'Mrs' is a contraction of what word?

3. What is the predominant colour of Venetian gondolas?

4. What is the Taylor family's neighbours' name in the television series 'Home Improvements'?

5. After humans, what animal causes the most deaths in Africa?

6. How many chambers are there in the human heart?

7. How many thousands in a million?

8. According to Bible records, who is the longest-lived man?

9. How many UK pounds are there in a kilogram?

10. What was the name of the boat wrecked on 'Gilligan's Island'?

General Knowledge Quiz #4—Answers

1. Shingles

2. Mistress

3. Black

4. Wilson

5. Hippopotamus

6. 4

7. 1,000

8. Methuselah

9. 2.2046

10. SS Minnow

82

Trodswow

IMXPS

TIME REQUIRED	SIZE OF GROUP	MATERIAL REQUIRED
No extra time required.	Unlimited.	Prepared overhead or flip-chart sheet.

Overview

Here is a very quick activity designed to show people that they sometimes tend to overlook the obvious.

Goals

1. To demonstrate that it is sometimes easy to overlook the obvious.
2. To energise the group.

Procedure

1. Show the word 'Trodswow' to the group.
2. Tell them that there are two words located inside it.
3. Ask them what they are.
4. When you get your first correct answer, give the person a prize for seeing the obvious.

Discussion points

1. Did anyone find other words inside? What were they?
2. Why do we sometimes tend to overlook the obvious?
3. Why do we tend to assume too much?

Variation

1. After point 2 in the Procedure don't say anything else. Wait and see what happens. People will assume that they are to find the two words, but in fact what you've done is made a statement: 'There are two words located inside it.'

Solution

If you haven't seen it yet, the two words located in the first word of 'Trodswow' are 'Two words'.

TRAINER'S NOTES

Trodswow

83

Team Effectiveness

TXLPES

TIME REQUIRED	SIZE OF GROUP	MATERIAL REQUIRED
30–60 minutes, depending on the size of the group and how much time the facilitator wants to spend on the exercise.	Unlimited.	Copies of the 'Team Effectiveness Questionnaire' and a pen for each person.

Overview

An activity that allows for reflection on a team's effectiveness.

Goals

1. To allow teams to improve their output.
2. To allow team members to communicate more effectively.
3. To allow team members to look at ways of improving themselves.

Procedure

1. After a brief discussion on team effectiveness advise the group that they are now going to be given the opportunity to look for ways of improving their effectiveness.
2. Give each team member a copy of the 'Team Effectiveness Questionnaire'.
3. They are now asked to spend around 15 minutes answering the 5 questions. This is done as an individual exercise.

4. When participants have completed the questionnaire, bring the group back together and ask them to share their comments with everyone else. This should lead to further discussion on ways of improving the team's effectiveness.

Discussion points

1. Did everyone agree with all of the comments being made? If not, why not?
2. What are the 5 most important points being made?
3. What are 3 things that we can do as individuals to improve the team's effectiveness?

Variations

1. Modify the questions to suit specific circumstances.
2. If time allows, the facilitator can collect all of the completed forms after point 3 in the Procedure. The comments can then be summarised and given as a handout for further group discussion.

TRAINER'S NOTES

This activity is most suitable for work teams.

Team Effectiveness (1)

Describe two situations your team has found itself in that lead you to believe there is a need for improved teamwork.

Describe two situations in which your team is working well together.

Team Effectiveness (2)

What makes the team work together well in these situations?

What can you see preventing or hindering effective teamwork in your team?

What can you do to improve teamwork in your team?

Birthday Card

P

TIME REQUIRED	SIZE OF GROUP	MATERIAL REQUIRED
10–15 minutes.	Unlimited.	One sheet of paper, a set of coloured pens or pencils, a pair of scissors and some glue for each participant. The group will need a number of magazines or newspapers to select from.

Overview

This activity should demonstrate some of the stereotypes that some people hold.

Goal

1. To see if anyone in the group harbours any stereotypes or preconceived ideas.

Procedure

1. Tell the group that you have just received a message over the Internet from Sam the Doctor, a distant relative. A relative of theirs, that is, not yours.
2. The message was a bit mixed up, probably due to a bad line, but it said that they would be here tomorrow to visit. The message also said that it was their birthday tomorrow.
3. Now ask the participants to produce a birthday card for Sam the Doctor using the materials they have been provided. Allow 10 minutes to produce the cards. This is to be done in silence.
4. After the cards have been judged, a discussion should now be led into stereotypes. How many people assumed that Sam was of a particular sex?

Discussion points

1. Who assumed that Sam was male?
2. Who assumed that Sam was female?

Variations

1. Use a different name or profession, ensuring that the name is not gender specific.
2. Depending on the time of year change the story and make it a Christmas card.

TRAINER'S NOTES

Card Count

TCMXPS

TIME REQUIRED	SIZE OF GROUP	MATERIAL REQUIRED
5–10 minutes.	Unlimited.	A deck of playing cards.

Overview

This activity will show participants how people will try to complete a task even if they don't have all of the information. It should also demonstrate how staff can become unmotivated even though they get the job done.

Goals

1. To allow participants to become involved in an order-giving, order-receiving exercise.
2. To demonstrate how important it is to impart all of the necessary information when a task is being delegated.

Procedure

1. Tell the group that they are going to be involved in an order-giving, order-receiving exercise.
2. Then ask for 5 volunteers.
3. Of the volunteers, one should be given the role of supervisor and the others the roles of operators.
4. Tell the supervisor (in front of the others) that their job will be to think of a number between 1 and 40. They are then to give this number to the operators.
5. Tell the operators that they are to display 1 playing card each whose values together add up to the number given by the supervisor. Do not give any further information at this point.

6. After some initial confusion let the group know that the aces have a value of 1, the court cards (J, Q, K) have a face value of 0, and that the number cards have their own face value.
7. Repeat steps 3 and 4.
8. Lead the group into discussion. Let them know that people will try to complete a task even though they don't understand all of the rules. Point out that it is the **supervisor's** responsibility to get all information before giving out tasks.

Discussion points

1. How did the 4 operators feel with the first part of this exercise?
2. How did the 4 operators feel with the second part of this exercise?
3. How did the supervisor feel?
4. Was it the supervisor's responsibility to gain all of the information initially?
5. How does this apply in the workplace?

Variation

1. Use another volunteer to give the briefing to the supervisor and the operators. This allows you the freedom to observe more closely.

TRAINER'S NOTES

86

Egg Yolks

IFMPS

TIME REQUIRED	SIZE OF GROUP	MATERIAL REQUIRED
No extra time required.	Unlimited.	A prepared overhead.

Overview

A simple exercise that can be used at any time during training.

Goal

1. To demonstrate that we can be hampered in finding a solution to a problem by the way the information is presented.

Procedure

1. Ask the group how much they know about proper English.
2. Show them the 'Egg Yolks' overhead, making sure the last line is covered.

3. Ask them which statement is correct. Should it be 'is' or 'are'? Ask how many are undecided?
4. Show them the covered line and tell them that they all wrong! Egg yolks are yellow, not white.

Discussion points

1. Why is it sometimes hard to solve problems like this?
2. Whose fault was it that not everyone got the correct answer initially?

Variation

1. Use any similar item.

TRAINER'S NOTES

Egg Yolks

Which is Correct?

- The yolk of eggs IS white?
- The yolk of eggs ARE white?
- Undecided?

- The yolk of eggs is/are YELLOW!

87

Roving Reporters

ITM

TIME REQUIRED	SIZE OF GROUP	MATERIAL REQUIRED
20–30 minutes depending on the size of the group.	Unlimited.	Pen and paper for each person.

Overview

An exercise to get people moving around the room and meeting others at the very start of a program.

Goals

1. To get individual participants to meet 5 others in the course.
2. To energise the group.
3. To find out more about the individuals on the course.

Procedure

1. Ask each person to take a piece of paper and a pen and write at least 3 interesting questions they would like to ask others in the group. Examples similar to the following may be given.
   Where were you when ...?
   What's your favourite book?
   What's your favourite movie?
   If you could have dinner with any person, living or dead, who would it be and why?
   What's the best thing that's ever happened to you?
   What's the most embarrassing thing you've ever done?
   Who's the most interesting person you've ever met?
2. Then ask the group to stand up and act as roving reporters. They must each interview 5 others, asking their 3 questions. Allow them 15 minutes for this.

3. After everyone has interviewed their 5 people call on participants to let the whole group know what the most interesting answers were to their questions.
4. Prizes could be given for the most unusual response and the most interesting question.

Discussion points

1. Who got the most unusual response?
2. Who had the most interesting question?
3. Were some questions easier/harder to answer than others?

Variations

1. The duration can be changed to suit the group size.
2. Questions can be prepared in advance by the facilitator and printed on handouts.
3. Can be conducted in pairs.

TRAINER'S NOTES

88

Late Starter

ITLPE

TIME REQUIRED	SIZE OF GROUP	MATERIAL REQUIRED
20–30 minutes depending on the lateness of the person and the complexity of the material.	Unlimited.	Your training notes, overheads and so on.

Overview

What do you do about a person who turns up very late for training? If you have a little spare time and would like to complete a great review, here's an idea.

Goals

1. To bring a late-comer up to date with the training.
2. To complete a review of the training to date.
3. To ensure that the group has understood everything to date.
4. To energise the group.

Procedure

1. When you have a late-comer arrive (very late, say a half-day or day late), ask the group to conduct a review session for them.

2. Give the group your notes and any training aids used, and then 5 minutes or so to prepare.
3. Allow the group free rein to present their review for the late-comer.
4. After the review has been completed, it is now your chance to go back and review any points that were a bit 'fuzzy'.

Discussion points

1. Was everything covered?
2. Can anybody think of anything else that was important that hasn't been mentioned?

Variation

1. This exercise can be used at any stage during training. You don't need a late-comer to prompt it.

TRAINER'S NOTES

89

Underwater Monument

TCXS

TIME REQUIRED	SIZE OF GROUP	MATERIAL REQUIRED
90 minutes.	12–20.	Prepared overheads of 'Atlantis Map', 'Possible Results' and 'Possible Solutions' (or handouts of these), and handouts of 'The Underwater Monument Exercise Briefing Sheet'. Each group will require paper and pens, thin sheets of cardboard, scissors, glue, ruler, felt-tip pens, flip-chart paper and calculators.

Overview

While this exercise looks at improving time-management skills it can also be used in many other areas.

Goals

1. To examine the value of planning.
2. To improve teamwork.

Procedure

1. Break the group up into teams of 4–5 people. Each team will represent the Atlantis Monument Building Company (AMBCO). Give everyone a copy of 'The Underwater Monument Briefing Sheet'.
2. Tell them that they have recently been approached by the King of Atlantis, who has not been well recently. He wants them to quote for building one or more pyramids to stand as an underwater monument to him when he dies. Like all clients he has a budget—10.5 million doubloons—and he is anxious that it be completed in his lifetime. He is 50 years old at present. The average life expectancy in Atlantis is just 60 years of age.
3. Show the group the overhead transparency with the map of the area. Show them that there are 2 quarries where the company can obtain blocks for pyramid building and 2 sites where the monument may be built.
4. Advise them that their job is to:
   - decide whether to build a single impressive pyramid or 2 smaller pyramids
   - decide which quarry to use for stone
   - decide which site to build on
   - decide the size of the pyramid/s

- calculate how long it will take to construct the pyramid/s
- calculate all associated costs
- build a scale model of their pyramid/s using the resources supplied
- write a sales slogan to promote their company
- prepare a 5-minute presentation to the King (the facilitator).

The time limit to complete these tasks is 45 minutes.

5. Tell them that will have a number of resources available to them. Tell them that they should aim to work as a team: the key resource is the other people in their team. Show them the other resources available.
6. Highlight the fact that the pyramid/s must have a square base and the sides of the pyramid should be the same length as the base line. Each angle of the sides will be 60°. However, there is no need for protractors—strips of card the right length can be used to find the correct position.
7. After completion of the building phase, each group is to give a 5-minute presentation of their results. The presentation to the King of Atlantis will incorporate the scale model constructed by the group and will show all calculations and any other details they feel are important.
8. Overheads (or handouts) should be shown giving 'Possible Results' and 'Possible Solutions'.
9. Lead a discussion into the areas of time management, planning, communication skills and so on, according to the outcome and areas needing attention. It should be noted in the debriefing that the team who spent the most time planning and organising had the best results.

Discussion points

1. Did anyone take control in each group?
2. What were your organisational skills like? How could they have been improved?
3. Was there enough time spent planning?
4. Were tasks delegated effectively?
5. How were the decisions made?
6. How successful were the presentations at the end? How much effort was devoted to this part of the activity?
7. How would you do it differently next time?

Variations

1. Use larger groups.
2. To look at leadership styles and delegation, give the briefing as a handout to one person in each group. Tell them that they are not allowed to show the other team members the briefing sheet. Everything has to be explained verbally.

Possible solutions

1. Site A
2. 90-pace pyramid (single structure)
3. Titanic Quarry
4. Costing 10.2 million doubloons

5. Taking 3,400 days or 9.32 years
6. Sales slogan: 'Live long, live on, in an AMBCO construction'

Alternatively, teams may wish to allow for a greater time margin for safety or a greater margin for profit. In which case:

1. Site A
2. Two 70-pace pyramids
3. Titanic Quarry
4. Costing 9.6 million doubloons
5. Taking 3,200 days or 8.77 years
6. Sales slogan: 'We pull harder'

If the swamp is deemed a threat to the work then the teams may select:

1. Site B
2. 70-pace pyramid (single structure)
3. Bismarck Quarry
4. Costing 4 million doubloons (under half the price, as per the company motto)
5. Taking 3,200 days or 8.77 years (even this period is pushing your luck with the seven plagues of ancient Atlantis)
6. Sales slogan: 'Better safe than sorry'

TRAINER'S NOTES

The Underwater Monument Briefing Sheet

Your group represents the management team of the Atlantis Monument Building Company (AMBCO) who specialise in monument building and selling. Your company motto is: 'Our pyramids are Cheops* at half the price'.

The King of Atlantis (who has not been well of late) has recently demanded that you submit a tender for the construction of one or more pyramids. His Eminence is looking for some sort of monument that will remind his people of him when he is no longer on Earth.

What he has in mind is square-based pyramids with equilateral faces. Because of the costs he is undecided whether to have a single impressive structure or a pair of smaller pyramids. He would welcome your advice on this matter, as he would on the choice of site. Should this be in a clear view of the palace gates or should it be five leagues south, at the site of the other monuments to his family?

The King suggests that (on pain of death) the costs should not exceed ten-and-a-half million doubloons. He likes value for money and wishes to impress his people with the amount he is spending.

He is now 50 years of age and he desires to see the completed structure. If this does not happen he will leave instructions that all the slaves who worked on the job—together with all members of the construction company—are to be entombed with him inside the pyramid when it is finally finished. Average life expectancy in ancient Atlantis is just 60.

Your task, then, is to submit your tender to the King in the form of a five-minute presentation. This should include:

- the site chosen
- the size of the pyramid/s
- the length of time to completion
- the total cost
- a scale model of the pyramid/s
- a sales slogan to promote your company and convince the King you are the best firm for the job
- any further points you feel are relevant.

Listed below are some other details you will find useful.

Labour force

Slaves work seven days a week. The only cost is the cost of feeding them. Regrettably, this is necessary or their efficiency drops markedly. The cost is half a doubloon per slave per day.

The total available workforce at any time is 1,000 workers. It takes 20 workers to move each block of stone.

Pyramid size

Length of side (paces)	Number of blocks required
70	80,000
80	120,000
90	170,000
100	240,000

Cost of blocks

Titanic Quarry = 50 doubloons
Bismarck Quarry = 30 doubloons

Transport time

(includes both transport and positioning of each block)

Bismarck Quarry to Site A:	3 days
Titanic Quarry to Site A:	1 day
Bismarck Quarry to Site B:	2 days
Titanic Quarry to Site B:	4 days

* Cheops is otherwise known as The Great Pyramid

Map of Atlantis

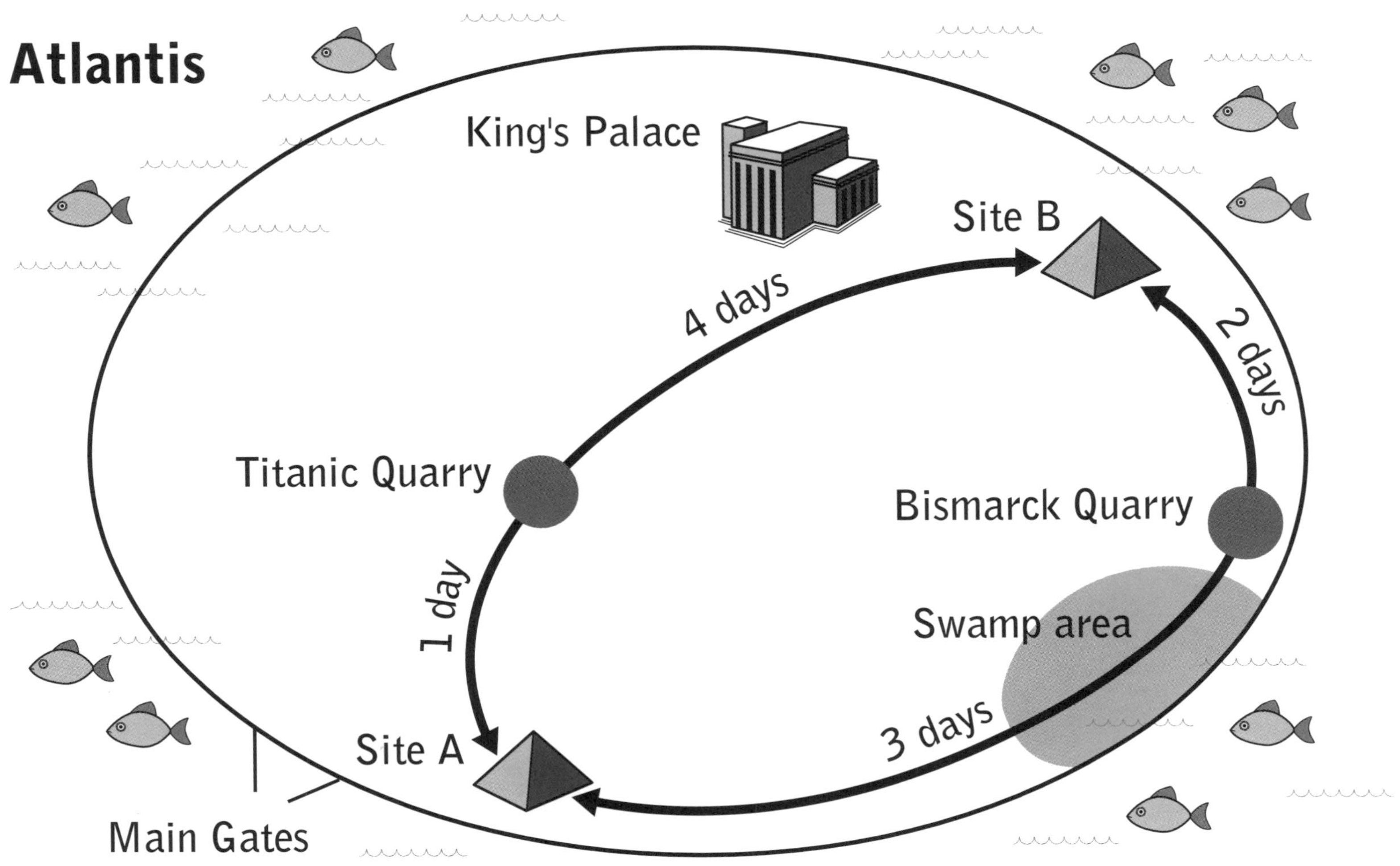

Atlantis

King's Palace

Site B

Bismarck Quarry

2 days

Swamp area

3 days

Titanic Quarry

4 days

Site A

1 day

Main Gates

Possible Results

Pyramid size	Site A		Site B	
	Titanic Quarry	Bismarck Quarry	Titanic Quarry	Bismarck Quarry
70 paces	4.8/4.38	4.8/13.15	7.2/17.53	4.0/8.77
70 paces (x 2)	9.6/8.77	9.6/26.30	14.1/35.07	8.0/17.53
80 paces	7.2/6.58	7.2/19.73	10.8/26.30	6.0/13.50
90 paces	10.2/9.32	10.2/27.85	15.3/37.26	8.5/18.63
100 paces	14.1/13.15	14.4/39.45	21.6/52.60	12.0/26.30

Key

Cost/Time

Sample calculation

Pyramid size   90 paces

Number of blocks required	170,000
Source of blocks	Titanic Quarry
Cost of blocks	170,000 x 50 = 8.5 million doubloons
Available workforce	1,000
Workers required to move 1 block	20
Numbers of blocks to be moved per day	1,000 ÷ 20 = 50
Total time to move blocks	170,000 ÷ 50 = 3,400 days
Cost of slaves	1/2 x 1,000 x 3,400 = 1,700,000 doubloons
Total costs	8.5 million + 1.7 million = 10.2 million doubloons
Time in years	3,400 ÷ 365 = 9.32 years

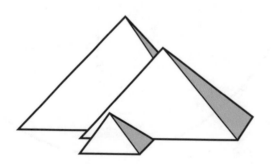

Possible solutions

1. Site A
2. 90-pace pyramid (single structure)
3. Titanic Quarry
4. Costing 10.2 million doubloons
5. Taking 3,400 days or 9.32 years
6. Sales slogan: 'Live long, live on, in an AMBCO construction'

Or, with greater margin for error and/or profit:

1. Site A
2. Two 70-pace pyramids
3. Titanic Quarry
4. Costing 9.6 million doubloons
5. Taking 3,200 days or 8.77 years
6. Sales slogan: 'We pull harder'

Or if the swamp is seen as a threat:

1. Site B
2. 70-pace pyramid (single structure)
3. Bismarck Quarry
4. Costing 4 million doubloons (under half the price, as per the company motto)
5. Taking 3,200 days or 8.77 years (even this period is pushing your luck with the seven plagues of ancient Atlantis)
6. Sales slogan: 'Better safe than sorry'

90

Nines

TCXLPS

TIME REQUIRED	SIZE OF GROUP	MATERIAL REQUIRED
5 minutes.	Unlimited.	Participants should have immediate access to pen and paper.

Overview

A quick exercise in problem solving showing the impact of urgency on quality.

Goals

1. To demonstrate how urgency can affect quality.
2. To show how easy it is sometimes to overlook the obvious.

Procedure

1. The facilitator asks the group 'How many times does the number 9 appear between one and one hundred?' Ask them to write their answers immediately.
2. Collect the answers and display them.
3. Lead a discussion into the impact of urgency on quality.

Discussion points

1. Why didn't everyone get the correct number?
2. How could we ensure that people come up with the correct solution?
3. How does this relate to everyday situations?

Variations

1. Any other number could be used.
2. Small groups could be formed. Tell them that this is a competition and the first correct answer wins. A discussion could then be led into the impact of urgency on quality.

Solution

The correct answer is 20:

9, 19, 29, 39, 49, 59, 69, 79, 89, 90, 91, 92, 93, 94, 95, 96, 97, 98, 99.

TRAINER'S NOTES

91

Salt and Pepper

ITM

TIME REQUIRED	SIZE OF GROUP	MATERIAL REQUIRED
10–20 minutes, depending on the size of the group.	Unlimited.	Prepared name plates/tents.

Overview

An exercise to get people who don't know each other mingling at the start of a program and to meet one other person.

Goals

1. To get individual participants to know one other participant on the course.
2. To energise the group.
3. To find out more about the individuals on the course.

Procedure

1. At the very start of the program ask each person to put their name on the name plate in front of them.
2. After this has been done ask them to turn their name plates over. They will find a word written under it.
3. They are now asked to find their 'other half' and talk with each other for a few minutes. An example of this is for the person with the word 'Salt' on their name plate to find the person with the word 'Pepper'.
4. When that has been completed ask them to sit back down and tell the whole group what they found out about the other person.

Discussion point

1. What did you find out about the other person?

Variations

1. Words can be changed to suit a particular group with similar backgrounds or professions.
2. Times can be changed to suit the group size.
3. Can be conducted in trios: Curly, Larry and Moe (the Three Stooges). Maurice, Barry and Robin (the Bee Gees), Franklin, Washington and Reagan (previous US presidents),. Willow, Oak and Ironbark (all types of trees).
4. The pairs (or trios) of words could be far more obscure or harder to match. This will lead to more discussion and laughter at the beginning.

TRAINER'S NOTES

If people pair up with the wrong partner, don't worry about it. Just get the leftover people to pair up randomly, this may lead to a bit of laughter during the introductions.

Salt and Pepper Pairs (suggestions)

Salt	Pepper	Happy	Sad
Bread	Butter	Surf	Board
Laurel	Hardy	Fred	Ethel
Pen	Paper	Merry	Christmas
Bill	Hillary	Fish	Chips
Apple	Orange	Barney	Betty
Cup	Saucer	Roy	Trigger
Lucy	Desi	King	Queen

92

Letters #2

IMXP

TIME REQUIRED	SIZE OF GROUP	MATERIAL REQUIRED
2 minutes.	Unlimited.	A prepared overhead.

Overview

A simple exercise that can be used at any time during training.

Goals

1. To demonstrate how the correct answer may not be the most obvious.
2. To demonstrate how a lack of time can cause wrong answers.

Procedure

1. Ask the group how good they think their English and numeracy skills are.
2. Show them the 'Letters' overhead.
3. Ask them to say which is most-used letter in this sentence.
4. Give the person with the first correct answer a prize.

Discussion points

1. What prevented us from all coming up with the correct answer initially?

2. How did the person that got it right do it?
3. How does this apply in the workplace?

Solution

The correct answer is 22.

22	Es
21	Fs
19	Os
14	Ts
13	Ss
12	Hs
10	Rs
9	As
8	Is
6	Ns
5	Ls
4	Cs and Gs
3	Ds, Ps, Us and Ws
2	Ks, Ms, Vs and Ys
1	B
0	Js, Qs, Xs and Zs

TRAINER'S NOTES

Letters

Facing famine if the crops were not safely harvested before the plague of locusts flew in, the farmer forgot to offer thanks to his five offsiders who had so often fought for the safety of his flock of sheep.

93

Apples and Oranges

MX

TIME REQUIRED	SIZE OF GROUP	MATERIAL REQUIRED
2 minutes.	Unlimited.	Prepared overhead or flip-chart.

Overview

A quick exercise to show that the right starting point is sometimes the least obvious one.

Goals

1. To allow participants to be involved in a simple problem-solving exercise.
2. To show how the right starting point is sometimes the least obvious one.

Procedure

1. Let the group know that they are going to be asked to solve a simple problem.
2. Tell them that you went to the market last night and purchased 3 boxes of fruit: a box of apples, a box of oranges and a box with a mixture of both. You were told by the vendor that all of the boxes that day were incorrectly labelled, although one box does contain only apples, one does contain only oranges, and the other box has a mixture of both.
3. Ask the group how you can determine the content of all 3 boxes by removing only 1 piece of fruit.
4. If anyone gives you the correct answer, reward them with an apple!

Discussion points

1. Why is a problem like this difficult to solve?
2. Why do we tend to overlook the obvious?

Variations

1. Use any 2 items instead of the apples and oranges.
2. Can be used as a small group activity.

Solution

By removing a piece of fruit from the box marked 'Apples and Oranges', we can determine its contents. If it is an apple, then the box marked apples must only contain oranges. Similarly, if it's an orange, the box marked oranges must contain only apples. The remaining box contains a mixture of both apples and oranges.

TRAINER'S NOTES

Apples and Oranges

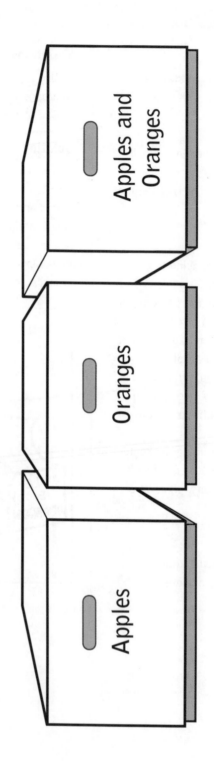

94

TX

Codewords

TIME REQUIRED	SIZE OF GROUP	MATERIAL REQUIRED
20–30 minutes.	Unlimited, but needs to be broken into subgroups of 5–7.	A copy of the 'Codewords Quiz' and a copy of the 'Codewords Solution' for each participant.

Overview

An activity to demonstrate the positive effects of teamwork.

Goals

1. To allow participants to be involved in a teamwork exercise.
2. To demonstrate the effect of synergy.

Procedure

1. Tell the group that they are going to be involved in a team activity.
2. Split the group into subgroups of 5–7 people.
3. Give everyone a copy of the 'Codewords Quiz' and tell them that they have to solve it.
4. Explain that the 'Codewords Quiz' is a crossword without questions. Every letter of the alphabet is used at least once, and every letter corresponds to a number between 1 and 26. Thus, A might be 1, B might be 2 and so on.
5. You could give them a start to the puzzle by telling them that number 3 corresponds to 'R'.
6. The group that finishes first should get a prize.

Discussion points

1. What helped you in solving the quiz?
2. What hindered you in solving the quiz?
3. How can we improve team problem solving?
4. How would you do it next time?

Variation

1. Use another crossword containing more relevant words.

Source: Airways, Qantas Inflight Magazine.

TRAINER'S NOTES

Codewords Quiz

25	1	18	3	19	21	19	22	25	4		3	25	19	22	6	18	3	9	24	8
1			8		22		25		19		18			18			3			
25	23	9	4	25	19	23	9		7	18	18	16	9	3	25		24	25	21	25
4		2		4		19		19	24			9		23		7	9			22
18		10		5	18	21	25		18	10	9	25	22	19	25		4	25	18	24
22	9	25	3			9		22	18		8		10		4			14
9		4		24		22			4			12		9		25	6	3	18
	8	5	14	13	18	18	22		10	18	22	12	19	10	8	24		3		3
15		14		9		2		10		22		25		13		13	9	25	8
2	8	8	9	3		24	9	25	24	19	23	9		18	22	9		9		25
16		2		3	25		22		25		22			19		9	23	19	8
1	2	24		5		14	3	18	7	4	9	23		10			18		19
2				9		9		19		9	12	9		8	9	16	14	18
10	18	10	18	25		18	22		24		25			25			22
17		3		8		14		25		16	18	12	9		25	26	19	18	16
	16	25	8	9		4	25	16	1		18		16		19		3		24
21		5			9		25		5	18	2		18			21	19	22
25		6		10			11			3	25	11	18	3		25		9
4	9	19	24	2	3	9		9	25	24	9		25		19	22	10	25
25		24		3		25		23		16		3			11		17
13		13	18	1	25	3	8		24	20	2	25	8	8	18	10	3	25	10	5

1	2	3	4	5	6	7	8	9	10	11	12	13	14	15	16	17	18	19	20	21	22	23	24	25	26

Codewords Solutions

A	B	O	R	I	G	I	N	A	L		R	A	I	N	F	O	R	E	S	T
B			T		N			A		I			O			O				R
A	D	E	L	A	I	D	E		W	O	O	M	E	R	A		S	A	G	A
L		U		L		I		I	S			E		D		W	E			N
O		C		Y	O	G	A		O	C	E	A	N	I	A		L	A	O	S
N	E	A	R			E			N	O		T		C		L				P
E		L		S		N			L			V		E		A	F	R	O	
	T	Y	P	H	O	O	N		C	O	N	V	I	C	T	S		R		R
J		P		E		U		C		N		A		H		H	E	A	T	
U	T	T	E	R		S	E	A	S	I	D	E		O	N	E		E		A
M		U		R	A		N		A		N			I		E	D	I	T	
B	U	S	Y		Y		P	R	O	W	L	E	D		C			O		I
U				E		E		I		E	V	E		T	E	M	P	O		N
C	O	C	O	A		O	N		S		A			A					N	
K		R		T		P		A		M	O	V	E		A	X	I	O	M	
	M	A	T	E		L	A	M	B			O		M		I		R		S
G		Y			E		A			Y	O	U		O			G	I	N	
A		F		C		Z			R	A	Z	O	R		A		E			
L	E	I	S	U	R	E		E	A	S	E		A			I	N	C	A	
A		S		R		A	D		D			M		R		Z		K		
H		H	O	B	A	R	T		S	Q	U	A	T	T	O	C	R	A	C	Y

Code

1	2	3	4	5	6	7	8	9	10	11	12	13	14	15	16	17	18	19	20	21	22	23	24	25	26
B	U	R	L	Y	F	W	T	E	C	Z	V	H	P	J	M	K	O	I	Q	G	N	D	S	A	X

95

Create a Game

TFML

TIME REQUIRED	SIZE OF GROUP	MATERIAL REQUIRED
45–60 minutes, but really depends on the size of the group and the designs that teams come up with.	Unlimited.	A prepared overhead showing the 'Game Names' and a copy of the 'Create a Game' handout for everyone.

Overview

A fun activity to get participants thinking, moving and talking. Generally to be used on a 'train the trainer'-type course.

Goals

1. To get participants thinking about game design.
2. To develop creativity within the teams.
3. To energise the group.
4. To develop a team spirit.

Procedure

1. Divide the group into smaller groups of 3–4 people.
2. Tell the small groups that they are now going to conduct a training course tomorrow.
3. The course content is up to them. However you are now asking them to design a game that can be used during a training session. They must select a game name from the list shown.

4. The game is to be no longer than 5 minutes in duration.
5. Give out copies of the 'Create a Game' handout to all participants.
6. After they have designed their games, they should introduce them to the whole group. If time permits they should also conduct them.

Discussion points

1. Who had the most interesting design?
2. Are any of them relevant to today's training?
3. Should we send any of these to the author of this book for inclusion in the their next book?

Variations

1. Tell the groups what their topic areas are.
2. Select a game name for each group.
3. The game titles can be modified if necessary.

TRAINER'S NOTES

Create a Game—Game Names

Astronauts	Nemesis
Bee's Behind	Over Board
Clowns for Sale	Pull the Other One
Decontaminate	Quickly Quickly
Elephant Ears	Roman Ruins
Flight Path	Sirius
Gallows	Titanic
Harmania	Uranus
Ice Berg	Vasectomy
Just a Minute	Warlock Wizardry
Knights of the Round Table	Xenon
Land-O-Mania	Yankee Doodle
Mega Millions	Zoom Zone Zillions

Create a Game

Name

Overview

Goals

Time required

Size of group

Material required

Procedure

Discussion points

Variations

96
Chips

ITS

TIME REQUIRED	SIZE OF GROUP	MATERIAL REQUIRED
No extra time required.	Unlimited.	A number of 'chips'. These can be poker chips, drafts pieces, cut-out cards etc. You will need one for each activity where you would like to give a 'reward' plus a few extra in case of ties.

Overview

Throughout this book I have suggested giving prizes to people. As it is not easy to do in some cases, here is a suggestion to give lots of 'rewards' but only one prize at the end of the training.

Goals

1. To minimise the number of prizes being given out during the day but still have the benefit of giving 'rewards'.
2. To develop a team atmosphere if used as a small group exercise.

Procedure

1. Before you conduct your first activity let the group know that you will be giving out chips as a reward to the person that gets the first correct answer for each activity during the training.
2. Let them know that they are to collect as many chips as they can during the course of the program, and the person at the end who has the most will be given a prize.

Variations

1. Divide the group into smaller groups of 5–7 people. Then advise them that they are to gain as many chips as they can during the training. The group gaining the most chips will then be given a group prize.
2. If lots of chips are to be given out, it may be fun to have an auction at the end of training. People can then bid for items using their chips.

TRAINER'S NOTES

Anything can be used as a prize for an individual winner, but keep prizes inexpensive. Group prizes need only be a bag of lollies or something else that might be shared around.

97

99.9%

IMXPES

TIME REQUIRED	SIZE OF GROUP	MATERIAL REQUIRED
No extra time required.	Unlimited.	Prepared overhead.

Overview

An activity that can lead into a discussion about quality.

Goal

1. To demonstrate that true quality means 100%, not 99.9%.

Procedure

1. Ask the group what they would consider to be an acceptable level of quality. Most will say around 99.9%.
2. Discuss this briefly with the group. When they agree that 99.9% would be acceptable, show them the 'Is 99.9% Good Enough?' overhead and show them what would happen if we accepted that 99.9% as a reasonable level.

Discussion points

1. What level would you now consider to be acceptable?
2. Can we have different levels of quality in different parts of the organisation?
3. Can we always achieve 100%?

Variation

1. Use items that are specific to the group or their company.

TRAINER'S NOTES

This exercise will have to be rewritten for different countries.

Is 99.9% Good Enough?

If **99.9%** is good enough then:

- a new born baby in Australia will be given to the wrong parents every day

- 7,630 mismatched pairs of shoes will be sold every year

- 29,315 pieces of mail will be mishandled every hour

- 133,335 documents will be lost by the ATO every year

- 42 landings every day at Sydney Airport will have problems

- 315 entries in **Webster's Dictionary** will be misspelled

- 58,600 credit cards will have incorrect information on the magnetic strip

- 12,000 income tax returns will be processed incorrectly

- 4,500 parts will fail in every Boeing 747

- 48,800 copies of **Woman's Day** every year will go missing before delivery

98

Missing Numbers #3

ITMXLPS

TIME REQUIRED	SIZE OF GROUP	MATERIAL REQUIRED
No extra time required if an individual activity; 5–10 minutes if conducted as a small group exercise.	Unlimited, but the more the better.	Prepared overhead.

Overview

A simple exercise to get the group thinking.

Goals

1. To get participants thinking.
2. To participate in a simple problem-solving exercise.
3. To energise the group.

Procedure

1. Let the group know that you are going to show them an overhead with a series of numbers shown on it. The numbers are 1 to 15, without 4 and 9.
2. They are to tell you where the 4 and 9 should go in the sequence, and explain why.
3. The first correct answer should get a prize.

Discussion point

1. If done as a small group exercise, was it easier to find the solution as a group?

Variation

1. Pose the problem to the individuals, let them think about it for 30 seconds, then get them to form small groups of 5–7 members. Get the small groups to come up with the correct answer. Then lead discussion into the effect of synergy.

Solution

The numbers are shown in alphabetical order, using the first letter in the spelling of each number.

Therefore the 4 and 9 should be located as shown below:

8   11   15   5   **4**   14   **9**   1   7   6
10   13   3   12   2

TRAINER'S NOTES

Where Do the 4 and 9 Go?

8	11	15
5	14	1
7	6	10
13	3	12
2		

99

Errors

ICMXS

TIME REQUIRED	SIZE OF GROUP	MATERIAL REQUIRED
No extra time required.	Unlimited.	Prepared overhead.

Overview

A very quick activity to demonstrate why we need to look at the big picture to get the correct solution to a problem.

Goals

1. To get participants thinking about the 'big picture'.
2. To energise the group.
3. To have some fun.

Procedure

1. Advise the group that you are going to show them an overhead with 4 errors on it.
2. The first person to identify all of them will get a prize.

Discussion points

1. Why is it that most people can't see all 4 errors?
2. What stops us from looking at the 'big picture'?

Variation

1. Use any other statement—perhaps something to do with the theme of the training.

Solution

1. 'Their' is spelt incorrectly.
2. 'is' should be 'are'.
3. 'erors' is spelt incorrectly.
4. The fourth error in the statement is that there are only 3 errors shown!

TRAINER'S NOTES

What Are They?

Their is four erors in this statement.

100

Trivia of Trivia

ITCMXL

TIME REQUIRED	SIZE OF GROUP	MATERIAL REQUIRED
2 minutes if used as an individual exercise; 5–10 minutes if used as a group exercise.	Unlimited, but the bigger the better.	Prepared overheads, pen and paper for each participant.

Overview

A trivia quiz for use as an energiser immediately before or after a break.

Goals

1. To fill in time while people come back from breaks.
2. To energise the group.
3. To demonstrate the effect of synergy if used as a group exercise.

Procedure

1. Tell the group that you are going to give them a quick trivia quiz to test their general knowledge.
2. Let them know that you are going to show them an overhead with 10 questions shown on it.
3. They will be given 2 minutes to write down as many correct answers as they can.
4. After the 2 minutes are up ask them to stop writing. (Make it as formal as you want.)
5. Show them the correct answers and ask them to check their own answers. They score 1 point for each correct answer.

6. After they have scored their responses ask them who scored 10. Then ask who scored 9 and so on until you get to the highest score. Those who score highest may be awarded a prize.

Discussion point

1. None if it is conducted as an individual exercise, but discussion could be guided towards synergy if it has been a group exercise.

Variations

1. Use different questions.
2. Use trivia questions that relate to the group or their company.
3. After point 4 in the Procedure you could break the group into smaller groups of 5–7 people. Ask them to combine their knowledge and see if the group can do better than the individuals. Show the answers and collect the individual scores together with the group scores for comparison.

TRAINER'S NOTES

The Trivia of Trivia

1. How many dimples are there on a regulation golf ball?

2. What is a funambulist?

3. Where is London Bridge located?

4. What were Captain Kirk's last words before he died?

5. What TV character once scored four touchdowns in a single football game?

6. On 'The Red Skelton Show' what were the names of the two seagulls?

7. What was the Bee Gees' original name?

8. What was Simon Templar's ('The Saint') real name before he changed it as a boy?

9. What was Dirty Harry's badge number?

10. How many ice warnings did **Titanic** receive the day that it sank?

The Trivia of Trivia—Answers

1. 336

2. A tightrope walker

3. Lake Havasu, Arizona

4. Oh, my!

5. Al Bundy

6. Gertrude and Heathcliff

7. The Rattlesnakes

8. John Baptist Rossi

9. 2211

10. 7

101

Recycled

ITCMXLPE

TIME REQUIRED	SIZE OF GROUP	MATERIAL REQUIRED
10–15 minutes.	Unlimited, but needs to be broken into smaller groups of 5–7 people.	One empty box of matches for each group along with pens and paper.

Overview

An activity designed to demonstrate the effect of synergy.

Goals

1. To look at the benefits of synergy.
2. To get the participants to work together.
3. To develop lateral thinking.

Procedure

1. Begin this activity by handing out pens and paper to each participant.
2. Once all people have their writing materials they are asked to list as many uses for empty match boxes as they possibly can. They have 2 minutes to do this individually.
3. After participants have completed their lists individually have the whole group split into smaller groups of 5–7 people.
4. When the small groups have been formed ask them to compare their individual lists with each other.

5. After the lists have been compared they are then to come up with as many ideas as they can (as a group) in the next 3 minutes.
6. Groups then compare the number of ideas generated as a group as opposed to the individual numbers.

Discussion points

1. Why is it that the groups generated more ideas than individuals?
2. What caused the extra ideas to come about?
3. What helped the group?
4. What hindered the group?
5. How can this apply to the workplace?

Variations

1. Use any other object if matchboxes cannot be found.
2. Use an object that the group/company are involved with.

TRAINER'S NOTES

Sample Observer's Sheets

The attached 'Observer's Sheets' are to be used as sample designs. They have been included as reference for you to design your own 'Observer's sheets'. It is important when you use observers that they know exactly what it is they are supposed to be observing.

By using a properly designed observation sheet you are ensuring consistency. You are also ensuring that all the points you want raised will be covered in the final discussion phase.

Observer's Sheet No. 1

It is your task to record what happens in chronological order. Record the time in the left-hand column, your observation in the centre column and who was involved in the third column.

Do not take part in the exercise, pass any comment or make any suggestions. The information you provide after the exercise will assist the whole group to discover things that are directly relevant to the way in which they operate.

Time	Observation	Name

Observer's Sheet No. 2

It is your task to record appropriate points under the headings listed below.

Do not take part in the exercise, pass any comment or make any suggestions. The information you provide after the exercise will assist the whole group to discover things that are directly relevant to the way in which they operate.

Was the exercise planned?

How was it planned?

Were people organised?

...ources used?

...ed?

...d?

...e take?

...e communication?

...recording?

Observer's Sheet No. 3

It is your task to record appropriate points under the headings listed below.

Do not take part in the exercise, pass any comment or make any suggestions. The information you provide after the exercise will assist the whole group to discover things that are directly relevant to the way in which they operate.

How was the exercise analysed?

Were people organised?

Were objectives set?

Were tasks properly delegated?

Were all available resources used?

How was the group led?

Were problems solved?

How effective was the communication?

How were alternatives discussed and evaluated?

What else was worth recording?

Observer's Sheet No. 1

It is your task to record what happens in chronological order. Record the time in the left-hand column, your observation in the centre column and who was involved in the third column.

Do not take part in the exercise, pass any comment or make any suggestions. The information you provide after the exercise will assist the whole group to discover things that are directly relevant to the way in which they operate.

Time	Observation	Name

Observer's Sheet No. 2

It is your task to record appropriate points under the headings listed below.

Do not take part in the exercise, pass any comment or make any suggestions. The information you provide after the exercise will assist the whole group to discover things that are directly relevant to the way in which they operate.

Was the exercise planned?

How was it planned?

Were people organised?

Were objectives set?

Were all available resources used?

Was the time controlled?

How was the group led?

What roles did people take?

How effective was the communication?

What else was worth recording?

Observer's Sheet No. 3

It is your task to record appropriate points under the headings listed below.

   Do not take part in the exercise, pass any comment or make any suggestions. The information you provide after the exercise will assist the whole group to discover things that are directly relevant to the way in which they operate.

How was the exercise analysed?

Were people organised?

Were objectives set?

Were tasks properly delegated?

Were all available resources used?

How was the group led?

Were problems solved?

How effective was the communication?

How were alternatives discussed and evaluated?

What else was worth recording?

Further Reading

Below is a list of publications that can be used as sources for more training games. This list also includes publications that contain some theoretical background behind training and the use of games.

All of the publications are valuable, but some are more relevant than others. The symbols shown to the left of the titles have been included to give the reader a guide as to the relevance of these books to our topic of training games. The key to the symbols is shown below.

Reference key

✪ Read this one and put it in your library; it's a great training games resource.

★ Read this one if you need more information or ideas on training games or other associated areas.

☆ Read this one if you've got nothing else to do.

While some of these titles are fairly old, remember that a game designed in sixth-century India (Chess), can still be very useful, and a lot of fun. Training games never die, they just get modified.

☆ BAKER, Pat, MARSHALL, Mary-Ruth, **More Simulation Games**, The Joint Board of Christian Education of Australia and New Zealand, Melbourne, 1977.

☆ ——, **Using Simulation Games**, 2nd Edition, The Joint Board of Christian Education of Australia and New Zealand, Melbourne, 1982.

✪ BISHOP, Sue, **Training Games for Assertiveness and Conflict Resolution**, McGraw-Hill, Inc., New York, 1977.

✪ BURNARD, Philip, **Training Games for Interpersonal Skills**, McGraw-Hill, Inc., New York, 1992.

✪ CARLAW, Peggy, DEMING, Vasudha, **The Big Book of Customer Service Training Games**, McGraw-Hill, Inc., New York, 1999.

★ CARRIER, Michael, **Take 5: Games and Activities for the Language Learner**, Harrap Limited, London, 1983.

✪ CHRISTOPHER, Elizabeth M., SMITH, Larry E., **Leadership Training Through Gaming**, Nichols Publishing Co., New York, and Kogan Page Limited, London, 1987.

★ CONNER, Gary, WOODS, John, **Sales Games and Activities for Trainers**, McGraw-Hill, Inc., New York, 1997.

☆ EITINGTON, Julius, **The Winning Trainer**, Gulf Publishing Company, Texas, 1984.

☆ ELLINGTON, Henry, ADDINALL, Eric, PERCIVAL, Fred, **A Handbook of Game Design**, Kogan Page Limited, London, 1982.

☆ **ELT Documents: Games, Simulations and Role-Playing**, The British Council English Teaching Information Centre, London, 1977.

★ FLUEGELMAN, Andrew (ed.), **More New Games**, Doubleday, New York, 1981.

✪ FORBESS-GREENE, Sue, **The Encyclopedia of Icebreakers**, University Associates, California, 1983.

✪ GREENWICH, Carolyn, **The Fun Factor**, McGraw-Hill, Inc., New York, 1997.

✪ HARSHMAN, Carl, PHILLIPS, Steve, **Team Training**, McGraw-Hill, Inc., New York, 1996.

★ HONEY, Peter, **The Trainer's Questionnaire Kit**, McGraw-Hill, Inc., New York, 1997.

✪ KIRK, James, KIRK, Lynne, **Training Games for the Learning Organisation**, McGraw-Hill, Inc., New York, 1997.

✪ KROEHNERT, Gary, **100 Training Games**, McGraw-Hill Book Company Australia, Sydney, 1991.

★ ——, **Basic Presentation Skills**, McGraw-Hill Book Company Australia, Sydney, 1998.

✪ ——, **Basic Training for Trainers**, 2nd Edition, McGraw-Hill Book Company Australia, Sydney, 1994.

★ ——, **Taming Time: How Do You Eat an Elephant?**, McGraw-Hill Book Company Australia, Sydney, 1998.

★ MILL, Cyril R., **Activities for Trainers: 50 Useful Designs**, University Associates, California, 1980.

✪ NEWSTROM, John W., SCANNELL, Edward E., **Games Trainers Play**, McGraw-Hill, Inc., New York, 1980.

✪ ——, **The Big Book of Team-Building Games**, McGraw-Hill, Inc., New York, 1998.

☆ **Oddities in Words, Pictures and Figures**, Reader's Digest Services Pty Limited, Sydney, 1975.

☆ ORLICK, Terry, **The Cooperative Sports and Games Book**, Pantheon Books, Canada, 1978.

☆ ——, **The Second Cooperative Sports and Games Book**, Pantheon Books, Canada, 1982.

✪ PFEIFFER, J. William, JONES, John E., **A Handbook of Structured Experiences for Human Relations Training**, Volumes 1–10, University Associates, California, 1975–85.

★ ROHNKE, Karl, **Cowstails and Cobras II**, Kendall/Hunt Publishing Company, Iowa, 1989.

★ ——, **Silver Bullets**, Kendall/Hunt Publishing Company, Iowa, 1984.

✪ SCANNELL, Edward E., NEWSTROM, John W., **More Games Trainers Play**, McGraw-Hill, Inc., New York, 1983.

★ ——, **The Big Book of Presentation Games**, McGraw-Hill, Inc., New York, 1998.

★ SILBERMAN, Mel (ed.), **The 1997 McGraw-Hill Team and Organisational Development Sourcebook**, McGraw-Hill, Inc., New York, 1997.

★ ——, **The 1997 McGraw-Hill Training and Performance Sourcebook**, McGraw-Hill, Inc., 1997.

★ TUBESING, Nancy Loving, TUBESING, Donald A., **Structured Experiences in Stress Management**, Volumes 1 and 2, Whole Person Press, Duluth MN, 1983.

★ ——, **Structured Exercises in Wellness Promotion**, Volumes 1 and 2, Whole Person Press, Duluth MN, 1983.

✪ TURNER, David, **60 Role-plays for Management and Supervisory Training**, McGraw-Hill, Inc., New York, 1992.

☆ VAN MENTS, Morry, **The Effective Use of Role-play**, Kogan Page Limited, London, 1983.

✪ VILLIERS, Peter, **18 Training Workshops for Leadership Development**, McGraw-Hill, Inc., New York, 1993.

✪ WOODCOCK, Mike, **50 Activities for Teambuilding**, Gower Publishing Company, England, 1989.

☆ WRIGHT, Andrew, BETTERIDGE, David, BUCKBY, Michael, **Games for Language Learning**, Cambridge University Press, Cambridge, 1979.

TRAINING INFORMATION

We offer a comprehensive range of training services around the world. If you would like more information on our training services, please complete the information below and forward it to us by mail, fax or email.

Name: _____

Position: _____

Company: _____

Address: _____

_____

_____

Phone: _____

Fax: _____

Email: _____

I would like more information on:

☐ In-house Presentation Techniques Skills Seminar

☐ Public seminar information for Presentation Techniques Skills Workshops

☐ In-house Training Techniques Workshops

☐ Public seminar information for Training Techniques Workshops

☐ In-house Time Management Seminars

☐ Public seminar information for Time Management Seminars

☐ Public seminar information on other subjects

Post to: Gary Kroehnert
                Training Excellence
                PO Box 169
                Grose Vale, NSW 2753
                Australia

Or fax to: (02) 4572 2200

Or email: doctorgary@hotmail.com